PLAYS FOR ENGLAND

by the same author

*

LUTHER
LOOK BACK IN ANGER
THE ENTERTAINER
THE WORLD OF PAUL SLICKEY

with Anthony Creighton

*

EPITAPH FOR GEORGE DILLON

PLAYS
FOR ENGLAND

The Blood of the Bambergs
Under Plain Cover

JOHN OSBORNE

CRITERION BOOKS, INC.
6 West 57th Street
New York, N.Y. 10019

The first performance in Great Britain of *Plays for England* was given at the Royal Court Theatre, Sloane Square, London, on 19th July 1962, by the English Stage Company. *The Blood of the Bambergs* was directed by John Dexter and the film sequence was by John Dexter, Desmond Davies and Tony Gibbs. *Under Plain Cover* was directed by Jonathan Miller. The décor for both plays was by Alan Tagg.

The cast for *The Blood of the Bambergs* was as follows:

WIMPLE	James Cossins
CAMERAMAN	John Maynard
LEMON	Billy Russell
FLOOR ASSISTANT	Barbara Keogh
BROWN	Glyn Owen
TAFT	Graham Crowden
WITHERS	Anton Rodgers
GUARDS	Tony Caunter, Jimmy Gardner
RUSSELL	John Meillon
1ST FOOTMAN	Charles Lewsen
2ND FOOTMAN	Norman Allen
3RD FOOTMAN	John Maynard
WOMAN	Avril Elgar
MELANIE	Vivian Pickles
ARCHBISHOP	Alan Bennett
1ST REPORTER	Robin Chapman
2ND REPORTER	Barbara Keogh
3RD REPORTER	Tony Caunter
4TH REPORTER	Constance Lorne
5TH REPORTER	Jimmy Gardner

The cast for *Under Plain Cover* was as follows:

POSTMAN	Billy Russell
TIM	Anton Rodgers
JENNY	Ann Beach
STANLEY	Glyn Owen
1ST REPORTER	Robert Eastgate
2ND REPORTER	Donald Troedsen
3RD REPORTER	Robin Chapman
4TH REPORTER	Tony Caunter
BRIDEGROOM'S MOTHER	Constance Lorne
BRIDE'S MOTHER	Avril Elgar
BRIDEGROOM'S FATHER	James Cossins
BRIDEGROOM	John Maynard
BRIDEGROOM'S BROTHER	Norman Allen
BRIDE'S FATHER	Jimmy Gardner
WAITER	Charles Lewsen
GUESTS	Barbara Keogh, Pauline Taylor

Number One

THE BLOOD OF THE BAMBERGS

A Fairy Story

CAST

WIMPLE

LEMON

BROWN

TAFT

WITHERS

RUSSELL

FOOTMAN

WOMAN

MELANIE

THE BAMBERGS

FOUR JOURNALISTS

ARCHBISHOP

ACT ONE

The Cathedral

ACT TWO

ACT ONE

*Before the altar of a large Gothic cathedral. In the wispy
yellow light of an empty cathedral, a boyish-looking, portly
man of middle age is staring up around him in well-groomed
humility. As a few hollow hammering sounds die away he
turns to the audience, coughs discreetly into his sleeve and
speaks in an easy, sober and confidential voice. Around his
neck, nestled against his ample silk shirt, is a small microphone. In his hand he is carrying a larger one. His name is*
PAUL WIMPLE. *In a corner, seated and leaning against some
scaffolding is a casually dressed, bearded young man about
thirty. Around his neck hangs a Rolleiflex, and he is lighting
himself a cigarette. He looks bored and exhausted.*

WIMPLE: Those sounds you heard just then echoing far,
far above my head here and dying away in the
secret corners of this great cathedral were
probably the last sounds we shall hear from
this place tonight.
(*There is a reverberating clanging of tubular
steel on stone and a muffled shout.*)
Oh no, I was wrong, someone else is still here.
That sound you heard was the strange muffled
noise of men working, working into the night,
whilst most of the country lies . . .
(*Another clang and more hollow shouts.*)
. . . lies sleeping, quietly, patiently and with

13

love—I think I may say, quite unselfconsciously, with love. They have been labouring into the night in preparation for the tremendous events of the morrow. For what they are doing is, indeed, a labour of great love, as great as that which impelled those men seven centuries ago when they applied their ancient skills and crafts to the building of this great cathedral for the remembrance of man and to the glory of God. For in a few hours' time—twelve and a half to be exact—and on this very spot, the moment which millions of people throughout the world have awaited with such expectation will arrive and two very famous people will be united in holy matrimony; and united amid all the pomp and splendour that a proud and grateful nation can provide on such occasions for her most illustrious ones. On this very spot where I am standing now—no, a little more to my left I think, if I am not mistaken. Anyway, I shall be talking to the Archbishop himself in a few moments and I have no doubt he will very soon put me right. But as I say, on this very spot where I am standing now, in the tremendous, rather severe perhaps, but tremendous hush of this great cathedral where kings and queens and noble princes are interred, where there is no man honoured who was ever mean—as a great poet once put it—in this place tomorrow, at a little past one o'clock we shall be privileged to watch the most solemn occasion in our national life—a royal wedding. Yes, Princess Melanie is to marry Prince Wilhelm or, as I think we might venture to call him, as they

14

all seem to do, at least in this part of the country, our Prince Will. Our Prince Will will —Wilhelm will—be the first royal bridegroom to have walked down this magnificent nave for over a year and what a thrill it is when we remember those many happy—and solemn— but happy occasions. It is well perhaps to remember them, for as I say, looking around me now, into the lofty recesses of this soaring, gaunt and ancient house of worship, it is difficult to believe that shortly this still, silent place will be the very centre of such glorious splendour, such colour and trappings, such grandeur and, yes, I think I must say again, such solemnity. The last arrangements have been made, the vast technical complications have been tied up. Television cameras have been hoisted into their resting places, the last workman has put away his tools and all that is left is silence—silence, that is, except for my voice. There is something strangely unreal about it all. Silence and space, but in that very space is something living, tho' it be silent. Perhaps it is even possible to hear it. If you listen carefully. If there is a place anywhere at all tonight where it might be said that this nation's heart beats it must surely be here . . . where I am standing now . . . but before we finally take our leave tonight, I should like you to meet some of the people who have been responsible for the arrangements of the morrow. Months of intricate planning go into these arrangements and tonight we have here just one or two of these people who have

15

dedicated themselves to this task. They range from, shall I say, the humblest—no, not the humblest, for his job is an extremely skilled one, no—rather from the proudest of living craftsmen to some of the highest in the land. First, I have with me here Mr. Charlie Lemon. Mr. Lemon is the foreman in charge of all the workmen, the workmen whose—work—we have heard going on or, rather, coming to a close. Mr. Lemon, it must be a relief to you to know that your part in all this is virtually over?

LEMON: Well yes, I shall be quite glad to get home and put my feet up, quite frankly.

WIMPLE: But you must feel a tremendous sense of achievement to have finished everything in time?

LEMON: Oh yes, I do.

WIMPLE: What exactly is it you have been doing?

LEMON: Well, mainly seeing to all the seating facilities, etcetera, and supervising the erection of spectators' stands outside the cathedral itself as well as many of the more important stands all the way along the route.

WIMPLE: I see, well that's certainly what you would call a very responsible job indeed.

LEMON: Yes, well, it is really, I suppose.

WIMPLE: Very responsible indeed. Tell me, Mr. Lemon . . .

LEMON: Yes?

WIMPLE: How long have you been engaged in these preparations?

LEMON: Oh, months.

WIMPLE: Months, really?

LEMON: Oh yes, months and months.

WIMPLE: And how many men are involved in this work?

LEMON: I have under me at the present time nine
hundred and forty-seven, that's if my memory
serves me right.

WIMPLE: Nearly a thousand men and what are they?

LEMON: What do you mean, what are they?

WIMPLE: I mean what do they do?

LEMON: Oh, there are builders, carpenters, electricians,
plumbers and all sorts.

WIMPLE: Craftsmen of every kind in fact, and all
working at top speed for months.

LEMON: Years, really.

WIMPLE: Years?

LEMON: Most of the men engaged in this type of work
are employed on what is in fact a more or less
permanent basis, although there was a falling
off a year or so ago after the Coronation, but
then it picked up again recently. Of course, as
you know we've had two funerals and one
christening, that is a lesser occasion for us of
course, on this side anyhow, but they are still
much more elaborate than they were a few
years ago.

WIMPLE: So you have been yourself a specialist in this
work for quite some considerable time?

LEMON: Yes, you could say that. I suppose about
seventeen years on and off. On mostly.

WIMPLE: That must be an almost unique record.

LEMON: No, no, I wouldn't say that. There are lots of
chaps, dozens I should say, who were in it
with me from the beginning, you might say.

WIMPLE: The beginning?

LEMON: Yes, from the beginning, the earliest beginnings

of the industry, from the time that it ceased
to simply be an ancient craft and became the
thriving, modern industry that it is today. You
see, when I started, it was never much more
than a part-time job, practically all casual
labour.

WIMPLE: And do you think, then, that conditions have
changed a great deal?

LEMON: Oh definitely, yes, most definitely.

WIMPLE: In what particular way, would you say?

LEMON: Principally in the—in the—in the——

WIMPLE: In the status of the individual workman, I
imagine.

LEMON: That's right, the status of the individual
workman.

WIMPLE: In the pride, in fact, of being employed in
such a vital, thriving and forward-looking
industry?

LEMON: Yes, I should say that, yes.

WIMPLE: And would you, for instance, recommend a
young man about to start his working life to
enter this industry? For example, would you
encourage your own son to go into it?

LEMON: I would, most definitely; as a matter of fact it
was my son who laid the carpet we're standing
on at this moment.

WIMPLE: Well, I must be careful where I put my muddy
boots then.

LEMON: Yes, my son is now chief assistant in charge
of all carpet laying arrangements.

WIMPLE: You must be a very proud man, Mr. Lemon.

LEMON: Oh yes, definitely. He has always been a good
boy.

WIMPLE: I wish you could see this carpet, ladies and

gentlemen, in the flesh as it were, beautifully laid with infinite love and skill.

LEMON: Always been good to his mother.

WIMPLE: I'm sure. And there is really nothing else you would rather have done in life?

LEMON: Nothing.

WIMPLE: Nothing at all?

LEMON: No, I think I can say that quite honestly and sincerely. Of course I am only responsible for one small section of the industry, but I think I can honestly say, in all sincerity, that in all the time in which I have been associated with it I have never been tempted to do anything else.

WIMPLE: One last question, Mr. Lemon.

LEMON: And what would that be?

WIMPLE: Is it true that the working hours in your industry are far longer than the national average?

LEMON: That *is* true, Mr. Wimple. That is true. But you must remember this. There is a very special benefit which . . . comes out of simply . . . the privilege of being a worker . . . in this industry.

WIMPLE: Yes.

LEMON: That is to say, Mr. Wimple, a man who has a special pride in his job, a man who knows that what he is doing makes a difference to the world he's living in, who knows he's making a vital contribution to the greatness of this country. That man is a happy man, Mr. Wimple, and a contented worker, and for why? I'll tell you for why. Because he is a fulfilled man, and how many people in these

19

troubled times can say that today?

WIMPLE: All too few, Mr. Lemon, thank you.

LEMON: (*warming up*). I myself, just in my section mind you, I have calculated that during the past seventeen years in which I have had the honour to do this job, I could have built, using the same materials and labour, you understand, twenty-seven secondary modern schools and one million two hundred thousand houses.

WIMPLE: Thank you, Mr. Lemon.

LEMON: Thank *you*, Mr. Wimple.

WIMPLE: Now, as I told you earlier, I am to have the privilege of talking with His Grace the Archbishop himself. In fact it was first arranged that we should have a filmed interview earlier today so that it wouldn't be necessary to impose too great a strain on him just before —the momentous events of the—morrow, in which, of course, he is, what you might call, the leading actor. Apart from the principals that is. Naturally. However, His Grace was unable to come and talk to me as we had arranged, owing to his overlapping commitments in which, of course, his religious, that is to say his *formal* religious activities must inevitably play a part. Well now, someone has just handed me a note saying that His Grace asks to be excused from our meeting tonight as he is still deeply immersed in the preparations for his own vital role. You might think that by this time such a thing would hold little terror for an old, experienced hand at the game but this, of course, is to *ignore*, or

20

at least to devalue, the overwhelming spiritual burden involved. As any actor will tell you, the three hundredth performance of *Hamlet* may well be the most trying and taxing of all. A familiarity may breed, not contempt, but despair. I am sure you will join with me in wholeheartedly wishing His Grace good luck for yet another first night. It is now, er, by my watch, eight minutes past twelve and according to our report here, the Prince is at this moment speeding along in his car to be in good time at his appointed place tomorrow. As he drives along in his powerful sports car —and the Prince is a very fine, skilful and fast driver, as I have reason to know, I have watched him on several occasions—as he drives along, I wonder what his thoughts are. Well, that we shall never know of course, but although he will need to keep his mind on the road, just like any other young man . . . he will, no doubt, *be* thinking . . . but that will be made a little easier at any rate as the Ministry concerned has cleared the entire length of the highway for twenty-four hours for the exclusive use of the Prince, the Royal Party and, of course, other guests. The man responsible for this operation is, as you may know, Mr. Ted Brown, the newly appointed Minister of Culture. We have been able to persuade Mr. Brown to talk to us for a few minutes on the eve of, what is you might say, his first big production. *He is* here with me now so I won't waste his time but ask you right away, Mr. Brown: you'd really call

21

this your first big assignment would you not?

BROWN: That is substantially correct. My Ministry as you know was only created by the Prime Minister a few months ago, shortly after the General Election.

WIMPLE: I suppose it would be true to say that the United Socialist Party more or less fought the Election on this very issue, on the creation of your Ministry.

BROWN: We did. Naturally I would not wish to indulge in anything like party politics on the eve of a joyous and . . . solemn . . . occasion like this, but it is certainly true to say that my Ministry and its function in preparing this occasion and all the others like it, is a direct result of a deliberate political programme. The policy was *hammered* out in our usual democratic way, the dissident minority was expelled and the resultant united effort——

WIMPLE: Yes, well——

BROWN: United——

WIMPLE: The thing I want to——

BROWN: United Socialist effort, I must add——

WIMPLE: Yes, as you say, these petty squabbles of political life——

BROWN: Ah yes—I think it must be said all the same.

WIMPLE: Up until a few months ago, this great industry was under the direct control of a few individuals appointed by the King personally and whose offices were hallowed by time and tradition. Mr. Brown, do you think that by making a Government department directly responsible, it will really lead to an improvement in what

22

has always been, up to now, a superb public service?

BROWN: Well, of course, that is a question we have been hearing a great deal about, and there is no doubt that it is one that has dominated the public interest and will probably go on doing so for some considerable time. Quite naturally, I am particularly aware of it as I am personally, not only the centre of the controversy, but I think I can say, without taking any credit away from the Prime Minister and my colleagues, I have been from the first, one of the architects of the whole policy.

WIMPLE: But do you think it will lead to an improvement? I mean, how will the creation of your Ministry affect the ordinary man in the street?

BROWN: Well, I should be able to answer that question, *but I have to say*, and I think it is not an immodest claim in the circumstances, that the reason I was chosen for this major post in the Cabinet . . . is that I am . . . well, the man in the street. I know him, he knows me. I know what he feels and I try to make damn sure he knows what I feel. Which is what I am going to try to accomplish now, Mr. Wimple, so that you can get on with your programme and I can get on with my job. As you said yourself, it is difficult to discuss this whole question without reference to party politics, but I will do my best.

WIMPLE: Your post was hitherto held by the Guardian of the King's Household, was it not?

BROWN: It was, and very ably indeed, by Lt. Col. Taft.

WIMPLE: Col. Taft was to have been with us by now,

23

Ladies and Gentlemen, but a report came through that he has been delayed somewhere on the—on the—highway. But we have every reason to believe he will be here very shortly so we may have an opportunity of talking to him. (*To* BROWN.) Would you say that Col. Taft is still making an important contribution to this solemn occasion?

BROWN: He most certainly is. I must be absolutely frank and tell you that I simply would not have known my way around during those first difficult months at the Ministry without Col. Taft. His experience, his infinite craftsmanship and his dedicated feeling for the job are unique—absolutely unequalled.

WIMPLE: So that the jobs filled by individuals like Col. Taft have not become in any way obsolete?

BROWN: Not at all, quite the opposite. We need people like Col. Taft as much as we ever have and what's more we still need many, many more like him. It is simply a question of changing the machinery. The old, private, simple methods just wouldn't do any more. I am sorry to keep saying it, but I am afraid I have to because a lot of people still go around creating the wrong impression, not only about my Ministry, but about the whole basis of the policy of this Government—simply because they will get hold of the wrong end of the stick.

WIMPLE: Yes.

BROWN: Listen comrades. Let's not beat about the bush. What is the position of this country in the world today? Where do we stand, what is our position, what is our special contribution to the free countries of the West? Wherein lies our strength? Wherein? There is no ignoring the facts any longer: we are hanging to the cliff face of morality and, what's more, we're hanging by our finger nails. This old country that was for so long a leader is, alas, falling behind in the race. As we look around at this land that once gave so richly and lift up our eyes we can only ask: from whence cometh our help? Well, let us face it, who's going to bother with us? The brutal fact is there is not going to be any help, not if we lift up our eyes to the hills or anywhere else. No, the only help we can look to is self-help. Now a lot of people think that by that we mean help yourself. Or, I should say, a few people—a few people who have always just been out for themselves. They only wanted a few people to help themselves. But we believe that everyone, without exception, should learn to help —themselves. And I am thinking particularly of the old age pensioners.

WIMPLE: Ah, yes.

BROWN: Who are fast becoming such a strong and important section of our community. Not only can we boast of having more old age pensioners than any other European country but there can be no doubt that the time is not too far distant when they will form at least an electoral majority.

WIMPLE: You have allocated, let me see, twenty-five per cent of all the seats along the route to old age pensioners, haven't you?

BROWN: I have.

WIMPLE: There has been a certain amount of strong criticism of this decision in various quarters, hasn't there?

BROWN: There has.

WIMPLE: And it has been suggested that in view of the large number of women, and particularly children, who get killed in these mass demonstrations of—loyalty and affection—it might have been wiser to have given priority to them.

BROWN: Yes, well of course, I am quite familiar with that argument.

WIMPLE: But you don't believe it has any validity?

BROWN: I do not. I think it is based on muddled thinking that is completely at variance with all our beliefs and way of life. It is, as we all know, a sad fact that these joyous occasions are always and inevitably accompanied by a considerable number of deaths. And I regret to say that these figures have been steadily rising. They even exceed the figures for deaths on the road—and you know how concerned we were about them. We thought *that* was a problem. However, this is the market price of progress and of civilization. It is inescapable. But, as regards my concession to old age pensioners, this matter has been given considerable attention by His Majesty's Government and I can tell you now, there is no question of our going back on it.

WIMPLE: You don't think that this privilege will cause widespread ill-feeling towards old people?

BROWN: There has always been widespread ill-feeling

towards old people. No, I am afraid that just isn't my philosophy. If so many hundreds of people are to be trampled to death, let the old people take their chance too, that is the argument. No, I say—certainly not. I believe that the old must be protected as well as anyone. However, let's not look on the gloomy side. Whatever the figures may or may not be on this particular occasion it's going to be yet another wonderful, heartwarming, magnificent ceremony. I don't deny that there are some dry doctrinaire old sticks around to complain about the gew-gaws. You will always get long-faced old grouchers like that. Why we used to have enough trouble with them in the old days of my own party before we slung them out. Before the United Socialist Party came into being that is. Puritans I suppose you'd call them. Anyway, I think we can safely say that they have never represented anyone but themselves and thank God, there's only a handful left these days anyway.

WIMPLE: So you're not anticipating any active opposition from your old political opponent?

BROWN: I am not. I believe that particular gentleman you are referring to has given up political life altogether. Besides I doubt whether we shall ever see him again in this country. No, you see, the trouble with such people is that they always misinterpret the Mood of the People.

WIMPLE: Or perhaps they interpret it too well. Ah, now here is Col. Taft. Good evening, Colonel.

TAFT: Eh? Withers!

27

WIMPLE: And with him, I think, is his *aide*, Captain
Withers.

WITHERS: Good evening.

(TAFT *and* WITHERS *look very agitated and
miserable*.)

I am afraid we have—we have—come to take
the Minister away from you.

TAFT: (*To Brown*). Will you be long, sir?

BROWN: Just a few minutes.

TAFT: Ah!

WIMPLE: (*To* COLONEL). You look as if you have had a
hard drive, sir.

TAFT: Good. What's that you say?

WIMPLE: We are unaccustomed to seeing *you* look
flustered in any way.

BROWN: In conclusion, comrades, I would just ask you
to remember this: our race is not yet run and
it is not yet lost. We have time. We have
ourselves. There was a time, for instance, when
the Roman Mass was a profound experience
in which all men were able to participate and
which united the Western World. What unites
the world today? Nothing. Everywhere there
is strife and disagreement but what unites *us*?
What makes this little proud land one? I will
tell you: what we in this country have
managed to do is to isolate—to isolate the
poetical element in our faith. We have been
able to reconstitute our lives. We have based
our socialism on a common shared experience.
We have found the poetical imperative. I do
not have to remind you how we had lost it.
But now it is found again and let us rejoice.
Good night. Oh, and don't forget, if you are

28

demonstrating tomorrow, don't, I repeat, don't, have that extra drink. If you are going to be loyal, be sober. You may save a life.

WIMPLE: Thank you, sir. And now that very colourful, dignified and familiar figure, Colonel Taft. Colonel Taft, whom we associate with many, many superb and historical moments in the past, and, who has indeed been largely responsible for them—Colonel Taft.

TAFT: Eh?

WIMPLE: Many people will probably be anxious to know your feelings tomorrow when you will, for the first time, be taking a back seat as it were.

TAFT: Back seat? What back seat? I don't know what you're talking about.

WITHERS: I'm sorry, Mr. Wimple.

(TAFT *goes to draw* BROWN *aside.*)

WIMPLE: Yes?

WITHERS: I'm afraid it's not possible for Colonel Taft to speak to you just now.

WIMPLE: Yes. Of course. Perhaps you, Captain Withers——

WITHERS: Please excuse me. (*He joins* TAFT *and* BROWN.)

WIMPLE: Well, there we are, ladies and gentlemen, we must bring now our programme to a close. As Colonel Taft and his *aide*, Captain Withers, discuss some last-minute details let me remind you that we shall be returning here tomorrow at twelve o'clock noon, that is and I hope you will be able to join me in witnessing what will surely be yet another . . . day of joy. Good night.

(WIMPLE *hands his microphone to a technician*

29

and with a curious and casual glance at
WITHERS *he calls out amiably——*
Nothing gone wrong?

WITHERS: Wrong?

WIMPLE: Yes, you looked a bit pale just now.

WITHERS: What could possibly go wrong?

WIMPLE: Yes, silly question, old boy. Good night.

WITHERS: Good night.

(*Left alone,* TAFT *and* WITHERS *stare anxiously at* BROWN. *He looks stricken.*)

BROWN: Good god.

TAFT: Tragic.

BROWN: Good god.

TAFT: Young life cut off——

BROWN: Does the Prime Minister know?

TAFT: Just like that.

WITHERS: No one knows yet except ourselves.

BROWN: But what happened for heaven's sake, what went wrong?

WITHERS: The road block outside the city——

TAFT: Straight into it.

BROWN: What on earth was he doing?

WITHERS: About one hundred and twenty, sir.

BROWN: But what did he think he was doing? He must have seen it—it was a precaution!

TAFT: Just like his father.

BROWN: We cleared the whole damned motorway for him.

TAFT: Reckless. Grandfather. Same thing.

BROWN: What else did he want?

TAFT: Only that was a big, wild chestnut. Threw him and kicked his brains in.

BROWN: Was he mad, or what?

TAFT: Out, rather.

BROWN: But who in hell let him drive himself up?

WITHERS: He insisted, sir.

BROWN: You must be out of your minds. He's killed three people in that car in the last eighteen months, and you know it even if no one else did.

WITHERS: You know how the public liked to see the Prince driving fast cars—the speed-loving Prince they called him.

TAFT: Hopeless horseman!

BROWN: I just can't get this into my mind. Is he really——

WITHERS: Instantly, sir.

BROWN: Good god.

(*They stand in the stillness of the cathedral, broken slightly by the heavy breathing of the bearded cameraman who has dropped off to sleep.*)

BROWN: (*passionately*). Oh, you brainless, bloody, reckless, royal nit!

(*His rage crumbles almost immediately to near tears.*)

TAFT: (*with contempt*). Mr. Brown, you forget yourself.

BROWN: Oh dear, yes. Forgive me, I didn't think what I was saying.

TAFT: I think we must remember who we are and our responsibilities at this moment.

BROWN: I was so upset I didn't know what I was saying.

TAFT: Naturally. A tragedy has happened. We must keep our heads, stifle our grief and decide what we must do.

BROWN: Tell me, what have you done with him?

31

WITHERS: He's outside.

BROWN: (*frantic*). Outside!

WITHERS: In Colonel Taft's car, sir.

BROWN: Car?

WITHERS: Yes, in the boot, sir.

BROWN: Boot! You can't leave a Prince of the Royal House in the boot!

TAFT: I was about to issue an order. Wimple's lot should have left by now. Withers, go and see and then instruct the guard.

WITHERS: Yes, sir. (*Goes.*)

TAFT: Look here, I suppose you realize what this means.

BROWN: Yes, another damn funeral. I haven't even ordered a new gun carriage.

TAFT: No, not that, surely, sir. I don't have to point out to you the essential significance of this tragedy.

BROWN: Quite honestly, I haven't managed to work it out yet. The implications are too tremendous.

TAFT: Exactly. They'll be looking for a scapegoat.

BROWN: Oh, god!

TAFT: There will be accusations, charges of negligence. Could bring down the Government.

BROWN: We baptized him and allowed the sky to open, we let the white dove settle on him and what are we left with in the end?

TAFT: Eh?

BROWN: The King can't last much longer.

TAFT: Afraid not.

BROWN: Good God, man, there's no one to take his place.

TAFT: Whose?

32

BROWN: The Prince's—Prince Wilhelm, of course.

TAFT: I am afraid I don't understand you, the line of succession is indisputable.

BROWN: You're really mad, Taft. Thank God we took over!

TAFT: His younger brother is his rightful successor and——

BROWN: Prince Heinrich!

TAFT: Prince Heinrich!

BROWN: Taft, Prince Heinrich is as queer as a cucumber.

TAFT: Queer?

BROWN: Yes, Taft, queer. You've been in this game forty years, haven't you?

TAFT: Sir——

BROWN: Ginger beer, Taft, pansy, one of *those*, cissy. *Compris?* Bent!

TAFT: Good Lord, young Harry.

BROWN: Young Harry, he says, he's as bent as a bloody boomerang!

TAFT: Bent, but do you mean——

BROWN: Well?

TAFT: Well—that, that he'd never get married?

BROWN: Married—tough luck on *that* poor kid.

TAFT: But surely, sir, for the sake of his country, his duty——

BROWN: Taft, I don't know who you talk to in your job, but has it never struck you as slightly odd, even for a young Prince, that he should divide his time almost exclusively between the barracks and visiting the ballet.

TAFT: Well, naturally I thought that going to the theatre was a bit eccentric.

BROWN: And the grace and favour lavished on all

those interior decorators and fashion
photographers?

TAFT: I always thought they were utterly unsuitable
companions for——

BROWN: Yes, yes, exactly. Well, there you are, you see,
it's been me, old Joe Brown, I've been the one
who has had to see that these things have been
kept quiet.

TAFT: I'd no idea.

BROWN: Yes, that's bloody obvious, isn't it? Anyway,
even if we can drag him up the aisle, who do
you think we could get to go with him? Have
you any idea at all how many eligible young
women there are left in the whole of Europe?

TAFT: Let me think, well, there's——

BROWN: Yes, you have a jolly good think because I
have.

TAFT: Well, it is difficult when you're suddenly——
Princess Mariana?

BROWN: Mariana?

TAFT: Yes, you know, the Stettin-Bambergs.

BROWN: Stettin-Bambergs? Nobody will speak to them
even in their own country.

TAFT: There's always Princess Theresa.

BROWN: They couldn't raise enough credit to put a
deposit on a T.V. set to watch the wedding.

TAFT: Well, of course, if it's simply money you're
talking about——

BROWN: You know it isn't. If it were worth it we'd
pay them anything.

TAFT: Well, then——

BROWN: It's no use, Taft. Do you think I've not gone
into it? Even if we could talk Prince Heinrich
into it there isn't anyone available who isn't

34

half dead, dotty or just plain unacceptable
outside a waxworks.

TAFT: Have you ever considered Isabella, the Grand
Duchess of——

BROWN: Yes, I have. She has to shave twice a day so
she'd be able to use the Prince's razor, seeing
that he doesn't have to.

TAFT: I think that's a very cruel, distasteful thing to
say.

BROWN: She wears a surgical boot as big as a suitcase.
Oh yes, she'd look great creeping up the aisle.

TAFT: But when the Prince succeeds, surely the
thought of his duty—to the Royal House, the
succession—he could, well, manage the once.

BROWN: He mustn't.

TAFT: But he'll be King.

BROWN: Or Queen.

TAFT: God, you're right.

BROWN: Heirs, Taft. There must be heirs. You know
—and Salmon begat Booze of Rachab; and
Booze begat Obed of Ruth; and Obed begat
Jessie; and with *these* two at least we could
have began the begat all right. Believe me,
we need to. Wilhelm may have been a long
drink of watery milk but that girl Melanie,
she'd have laid eggs like a cod-fish.

TAFT: I say, poor girl, what's going to happen to
her now?

BROWN: (*sadistically*). Well, there'll be no performance
for her tomorrow, *or* tomorrow night for that
matter.

TAFT: But there is got to be—I——

BROWN: I know what you mean, old man, I'm sorry
I barked at you.

35

TAFT: No, not at all.

BROWN: But what can we do with her? This really looks like the end.

(*The body of* PRINCE WILHELM *is brought in by the guards, accompanied by* WITHERS. *It is placed in the centre of the stage. They all stare at it in silence and one by one go to look at it.*)

TAFT: (*roughly*). Well, there it is, the blood royal.

(WITHERS *is the first to look at the* PRINCE. *While the others do the same he stares at the sleeping figure of the bearded cameraman. He goes over to him and examines him.*)

BROWN. Yes, it's the end all right. The end of everything as we know it.

TAFT: Bamberg blood. Well, we'd better keep him out of sight for the moment. (*To* GUARD.) You—cover him up—put him over there. We've got to think, and think pretty hard.

BROWN: We might as well face up to it, Taft, it's all over. A big dream, a great idea, no . . .

TAFT: Oh, damn it, man, take hold of yourself for heaven's sake. Try and remember you're still one of His Majesty's ministers. If you tell me what to do I promise I'll carry it out.

WITHERS: Colonel Taft, sir.

TAFT: What is it?

WITHERS: There's a man over here.

TAFT: What, where, where is he?

BROWN: A man. Oh, my God, he's been listening.

TAFT: Good heavens, you're panicking again. Sit down for a moment. Let me look at him.

TAFT: Do you think he is really asleep?

WITHERS: Either that or drunk, sir. A bit of both, I should say.

36

TAFT: Withers.

WITHERS: Yes, sir.

> (TAFT *leans right down and examines the man more closely*.)

TAFT: Withers, have you noticed——

WITHERS: Yes I have.

TAFT: Am I mad?

WITHERS: No sir, absolutely not.

TAFT: It's fantastic.

WITHERS: I know, I couldn't believe it myself. That's why I waited.

TAFT: What a resemblance!

WITHERS: The Bamberg nose, the Bamberg ears . . .

TAFT: Why, shave off that hideous beard and, and——

WITHERS: Prince Wilhelm, sir.

TAFT: The Prince.

WITHERS: Dressed as a cameraman.

TAFT: I wonder what his chin is like.

WITHERS: (*encouragingly*). Bearded men always have feeble chins, sir.

TAFT: That's why he grew it, I suppose.

WITHERS: Exactly, sir.

> (BROWN *moans*.)

WITHERS: What are we going to do with the Minister, sir?

TAFT: Ah, yes. Well, I think we should collect our thoughts a bit, don't you. Get rid of him, put him in my car and tell him to go straight to the palace and get himself a brandy or something. We'll fetch him later.

WITHERS: Yes, sir.

> (*He goes to* BROWN *and helps him up*.)

TAFT: Oh, and tell him to talk to no one, understand, no one.

WITHERS: Yes, Colonel Taft.

(BROWN *takes a last look at the corpse and is helped out by* WITHERS. TAFT *leans down again and studies the man's features in detail. Suddenly the man opens his eyes.*)

TAFT: (*startled*). Oh!

MAN: Phew! (*Pause.*) I don't know what *you're* yelling about, *you* scared *me*.

TAFT: I beg your pardon.

MAN: You can kill people like that, you know. If I had a weak heart you might have killed me.

TAFT: Yes, well, thank God, I didn't. Who are you?

MAN: I think I might ask you that except, except that I know who you are. You're Colonel Taft. I've had enough trouble with your office too many times not to know you.

TAFT: Come along, man, don't mess about. Who are you?

MAN: Are you asking for my press card?

TAFT: Yes, please.

MAN: Just as you like. (*Goes to pocket.*) I've got every right to be here, you know.

TAFT: What were you doing here?

MAN: I should have thought you'd have noticed that.

TAFT: Yes, I mean before.

MAN: I was setting up my cameras. For one thing, you boys wouldn't let me in until it was nearly too late, so I had a few drinks while I was kept hanging around, thanks to you again, and by the time I had been allowed to set up I just felt so flaked out, I sat down for a smoke and dropped off.

TAFT: (*reading*). Alan Russell. Photographer— Australian United Press. Are these the people you work for?

RUSSELL: Only on this one. I work for myself.

TAFT: Come over here a minute will you, please.

RUSSELL: What do you mean, I'll be finished in a couple of minutes. You don't have to throw your weight around, you know.

TAFT: Do shut up for a minute, man. Come in the light where I can see you.

(RUSSELL *allows himself to be shifted into the light and peered at.*)

RUSSELL: Top lighting makes me look better but it's not very good in here.

TAFT: It's good enough.

(*Enter* WITHERS.)

Withers, look, look at him.

(WITHERS *comes up and examines* RUSSELL.)

WITHERS: Remarkable, absolutely remarkable.

(RUSSELL *looks puzzled but slightly amused. He is a good-humoured man.*)

RUSSELL: If I smoke will it spoil your view?

TAFT: What? No, certainly.

(WITHERS *smartly offers* RUSSELL *a cigarette.*)

RUSSELL: Oh, thank you. Must be quite a strain for you boys, a job like this.

TAFT: Mr. Russell, where do you come from?

RUSSELL: Well, I've shown you my card. Australia.

TAFT: Yes, but has your family always lived in Australia?

RUSSELL: Pretty well, I suppose.

TAFT: I mean, do you have any family connections in Europe?

RUSSELL: Sure.

TAFT: Look, Russell, what does the name Bamberg mean to you?

RUSSELL: Just about what it does to you I should say.

39

TAFT: Nothing more?

RUSSELL: Well, I used to think it was a bit of a joke when I was a kid.

TAFT: A joke, what kind of a joke?

RUSSELL: Well, you see, Bamberg was a name I often used to hear when I was a little kid. Sometimes I'd hear my old man rowing with my mother and somehow that name was always coming up and whenever it did, sure enough my mother would end up in tears and poor old Dad would storm out of the house.

TAFT: Go on.

RUSSELL: The last time I saw him, just before he died, I heard him shouting: "There you are, you see, that's your son, there's the bloody Bamberg coming out in him!" I'd just been sick on the bathroom floor and on that particular occasion I wasn't sure if he'd said Hamburg or hamburger or something. My mother's family came from somewhere near Hamburg, you see.

TAFT: Hamburg, yes.

RUSSELL: So it was a bit confusing, especially at the time.

TAFT: Did you ever ask your mother about Bamberg?

RUSSELL: Well I didn't, as a matter of fact, until after Dad died. Because, well, the name seemed to upset him too much and I didn't like to ask, but later I did say to her one day: "Who is this Mr. Bamberg?"

TAFT: What did she say to that?

RUSSELL: She said: "He was a very dear friend of your mother's when she was on holiday in Europe once."

TAFT: When was this?

RUSSELL: What Bamberg? The holiday? Oh, just before she got married, I think.

TAFT: (*to* WITHERS). It is, it is.

WITHERS: What was your mother's name?

TAFT: Walters?

RUSSELL: Walters—how did you know my mother's name?

TAFT: I remember her. She was a pretty little thing, blonde, very blonde. That's why I remember her. She was the only blonde he ever had. It was a relief after all those pasty-looking brunettes and red-heads.

RUSSELL: This job's really gone to your heads, I think.

TAFT: I apologize, Mr. Russell. You shall have an explanation. Come over here.
(*He takes* RUSSELL *to the body*, C. WITHERS *uncovers it.*)

RUSSELL: Phew! Oh, I say, what about that, eh? You boys are in trouble, I guess.
(*Both men are watching* RUSSELL.)
Gosh, he's a mess, isn't he. You know, I never realized he'd got such big ears. Yes—hey, you know, put a beard on him and he'd look a bit like me.
(TAFT *nods to* WITHERS.)

WITHERS: Mr. Russell, would you mind coming with me?

RUSSELL: Why? Where?

WITHERS: Oh, just to the Palace.

RUSSELL: To the Palace, what for?

WITHERS: For a shave, Mr. Russell, for a shave.

CURTAIN

End of Act One

41

ACT TWO

Scene 1

A room in the palace. RUSSELL, *clean shaven and wearing full dress uniform with sword and decorations, is kneeling before a long mirror.* WITHERS *and* TAFT *look on.*

RUSSELL: Hey! But do I have to stay on my knees all this time?

TAFT: Oh, don't grumble any more for heaven's sake.

WITHERS: There'll be a faldstool, your Royal Highness.

RUSSELL: A what?

WITHERS: A cushion.

RUSSELL: Grumble, he says! I should think I've got something to grumble about. I can't keep my eyes open.

WITHERS: Have some more black coffee. (*He rings.*)

TAFT: Good heavens, man! What's the matter with you?

RUSSELL. A good question. I can't remember my lines, and I can't stop this bloody sword swinging between my legs.

TAFT: Where's your manhood?

RUSSELL: Doing all right till this morning, thank you, mate.

WITHERS: (*encouragingly*). You're doing splendidly. Another couple of times through the whole

42

ceremony and you'll be perfect. You only
forgot three things last time.

TAFT: Those three were enough to bring the country
to a standstill.

RUSSELL: Well, as far as I'm concerned, you can send
for somebody else.

TAFT: There *is* no one else.

RUSSELL: Look: I'm not used to giving orders to a
butler, let alone being a royal bridegroom.

WITHERS: Don't worry, old man. I'll get the Archbishop
to cue you in all the way through. He can get
him through it. I'll say you've got a bad
attack of first-night nerves. (*To* TAFT.)

RUSSELL: First night—don't talk to me about *that*!

TAFT: (*grimly*). No, I should wait till you come to it,
my friend.

RUSSELL: *If* I come to it. My friend, you're no friend to
me. You'd better get yourself another boy.

TAFT: I've told you: it's you or nothing.

RUSSELL: Then it'll have to be nothing, that's all. I'm
certainly not marrying a princess I've never
even been introduced to.

TAFT: It won't be nothing, Russell, because I shan't
let it be nothing. There's too much at stake.
I'm warning you. You are unimportant to me.
You are nobody. As I am. As we all are.

RUSSELL: Are you threatening me?

TAFT: If you wish.

RUSSELL: Listen, all I've got to do is holler and get out
of here.

TAFT: (*quietly*). You'll not get out alive.
(*He takes out a revolver.*)

RUSSELL: You're mad.

TAFT: Maybe. I've been living in a mad world for a

43

long time. Longer than either of you.

(*There is a knock at the door.* TAFT *puts away his pistol unhurriedly. A footman enters.*)

WITHERS: His Royal Highness would like another pot of black coffee.

(*The footman bows and goes out. There is a tense pause.*)

TAFT: I'm sorry, Russell.

RUSSELL: That's all right. (*To* WITHERS.) Would he have done it?

(WITHERS *nods.*)

TAFT: I was overcome.

RUSSELL: Sure.

TAFT: There is so much at stake. For all of us. Think again, my dear chap. Please think again. Don't be hasty.

RUSSELL: All right.

TAFT: An entire world is involved. All that we have left. It's precious little.

RUSSELL: I'm beginning to see that.

TAFT: You're not a man to be threatened.

RUSSELL: Or bribed?

TAFT: Just think—think of the responsibility that lies in your hands at this moment.

RUSSELL: Well?

TAFT: A whole way of life. We are its servants, instruments of order, decency and all the things that have made life honourable and tolerable for a thousand years.

RUSSELL. I need time to think about it.

TAFT: There isn't any time. And the one thing you mustn't do is think. You must act, and *be* what you are.

RUSSELL: I've never had to make that decision.

44

TAFT: Make it now.

RUSSELL: How much longer have we got?

WITHERS: Six hours and twenty-two minutes.

RUSSELL: All right, then, let's go through the drill again. From the top.

WITHERS: I should wait for your coffee, Your Royal Highness.

TAFT: Yes, yes, take a rest for a bit. You've time yet. We'll get through.

(*A knock at the door. The* FOOTMAN *enters with coffee.*)

WITHERS: Ah, here we are. Get this lot down—Your Royal Highness. Is there anything else you'd like?

RUSSELL: Eh? No. Oh yes, I think I will. I'll have, I'll have a bottle of brandy and some soda.

TAFT: (*under breath*). Careful now.

RUSSELL: And, and—don't go. It's getting light. I might as well eat while I'm at it. I think I'll have bacon and eggs.

FOOTMAN: Very good, Your Royal Highness.

RUSSELL: And toast and marmalade.

TAFT: Excellent idea. We'll all have some.

RUSSELL: Good.

WITHERS: (*to* FOOTMAN). Soon as you can.

FOOTMAN: I'll have to wake——

RUSSELL: Then wake 'em! Wake the lot! It's my god-dam wedding day, is it not?

(*The* FOOTMAN *bows and goes out.* TAFT *and* WITHERS *exchange relieved glances.*)

WITHERS: Well now, that sounds better!

RUSSELL: I'm not convinced, mind. But I'm interested.

TAFT: Good man!

RUSSELL: Or I'm prepared to be. Interest me.

(TAFT *glares at him outraged.*)

TAFT: Interest you! Good heavens, man, we're not selling you a spin dryer or something.

RUSSELL: You'd better start trying.

TAFT: Damn it, you're being offered one of the—of the purest, most perfect pearls of living. It's like redemption, it can't be bought or bargained for. It is impossible to offer you anything more valuable.

RUSSELL: At a price.

TAFT: What do you mean, price? What price?

RUSSELL: Well, my freedom for instance.

TAFT: Freedom? *Your* freedom? What's that worth precisely?

RUSSELL: At this moment, precisely, I'd say its market value had never been higher.

TAFT: Damn your freedom, man. You can live without that. Tell me: what about duty? Eh? What about duty? That's harder to live without.

RUSSELL: (*baffled for the moment*). What about—work?

TAFT: Her Royal Highness will be your work.

RUSSELL: Yes, well. Maybe she'll be *too* hard work.

TAFT: She's exacting.

RUSSELL: But how satisfying?

TAFT: There'll be rewards. More than you ever got before.

RUSSELL: I wish you wouldn't say "got before" like that.

TAFT: Well, come along, my friend, let's be frank. You're not a great artist or something, someone who's work is so important to them.

RUSSELL: No. That's quite true. But I'm good at it.

TAFT: But no more.

RUSSELL: And I enjoy it. Still, I daresay they'd manage
without me.

TAFT: Come: a princess is more than a fair return
for *that*.

RUSSELL: We'll come round to her later. What do I get?

TAFT: Get?

RUSSELL: Loot.

TAFT: Eh?

WITHERS: He wants a breakdown, sir, of the Prince's
personal fortune.

RUSSELL: And the Princess's.

TAFT: Oh, do come along!

RUSSELL: Oh, all right. By the way, I warn you: I can't
get on a horse, shoot, play polo, or handle a
yacht.

WITHERS: Oh lord!

RUSSELL: Nor am I prepared to.

TAFT: Rubbish! You'll have to.

RUSSELL: I might, however, open the occasional industrial
exhibition, or launch an obsolete ocean liner.
You know, I've always wanted to crack a bottle
of champagne against one of those things.
(TAFT *looks as if he might take out his revolver
again.*)

WITHERS: I'm glad you're beginning to come round to
our point of view. You see, Russell—Your
Royal Highness—your personal fortune at this
time is not vast, although by the standards of
most men, it is very considerable.

RUSSELL: How much?

WITHERS: In your private purse, probably no more than
a quarter of a million——

RUSSELL: Is that all?

WITHERS: Your income, however, added to the Princess's,

47

would be very large indeed.

RUSSELL: How much?

TAFT: Withers!

WITHERS: Well, as a full-time, working Prince of the Royal House, you will naturally have an allowance from the public purse.

TAFT: Reviewable annually by Parliament.

WITHERS: After an event such as your wedding, they will almost certainly do something ordinarily unpopular, like cutting the schools programme and *increase* your allowance.

RUSSELL: Good.

WITHERS: And at such time as the Princess should produce an heir, there would be similar arrangements.

RUSSELL: Excellent.

WITHERS: Your father, as you may know, was a friendly, dissolute man who squandered a vast sum of money before he died, mostly on horses and opera singers—an especially rich product of your *own* country, I believe. Your *mother*, however, was a sensible thrifty woman, who, apart from furnishing all your royal residences at wisely invested expense (and with *monumental* vulgarity) made the widest possible provision for any of her sons who might follow in their father's footsteps. All Your Royal Highness's capital has been shrewdly invested in a large number of places, all of them assured, safe and profitable. Apart from your mother's stupendously valuable collection of antique junk, with which, however, you will be compelled to live, there is her jewellery, considered to be beyond value; your collection of paintings,

from Holbein to Sickert, most of them rather
dull but priceless, which has been recently
valued by one popular newspaper at nearly two
million pounds. You have a royal residence in
the capital, of course, which is rather like an
enormous version of one of the older, famous,
Edwardian hotels. You have a seat in the
provinces which is reasonably comfortable.
The weather is not good usually, and you will
have to stride about in a thick rubber
macintosh and gum boots, which will make
you popular with one certain, unconsidered
section of the population. Twice on Sundays,
you will go to the local church, and sit intermin-
ably in your pew with the rest of the crowded
congregation to prove how democratic you are.
It is a little like attending one of the flashier
film premières in a small village, but you will
soon learn to accept it as part of your country
life time table. You also own a huge Gothic
obscenity in the north, which is like a plush
railway station with William Morris wallpaper.
But it's very popular with the people, so you
are obliged to visit it during the summer, when
you're expected to dress in the very quaint
local costume, and pretend that you are not
yourselves foreigners. This is to encourage the
inhabitants of that sentimentally fierce province
not to insist on their sovereignty, which they
are very relieved not to have to do anyway. For
this service, the Government pays the whole
crippling upkeep of the place, and bribes you
in return for your claustrophobic and overwhelming boredom.

49

RUSSELL: Go on.

WITHERS: In addition to this, you're one of the nation's greatest landowners, the richest of large-scale farmers and breeders and racehorse owners—all at no effort to yourself. You derive income and increments from ancient lands, sources and foundations that everyone but the dustiest bookkeepers had forgotten. In short, Your Royal Highness, you are good and loaded.

RUSSELL: Yes. I see.

(*He plays absently with his sword. Pause.*)

TAFT: Well?

RUSSELL: Well——

(FOOTMAN *enters with a trolley.*)

RUSSELL: I suppose I'd better take a look at her.

TAFT: Take . . . !

RUSSELL: I mean I ought to see what it is exactly I'm getting.

WITHERS: (*to* FOOTMAN). Leave that for the moment.

RUSSELL: After all, I've only seen her on newsreels——

FOOTMAN: Yes, sir.

WITHERS: Ah, but she's damaged her fetlock since then, Your Royal Highness. She's not the same animal.

TAFT: Quite.

(*Exit* FOOTMAN.)

TAFT: Now, look here, Russell——

RUSSELL: I tell you—no see, no deal.

TAFT: There's no time.

RUSSELL: I only want to talk to her for five minutes. After all, I'm the one who's going to be stuck with her. Besides, she may not fancy the idea herself.

TAFT: The Princess has been brought up all her life

50

with an immaculate understanding of duty and
honour. She'll not shirk her responsibilities.

RUSSELL: Well, I might shirk mine. Have you told her
yet?

TAFT: No.

RUSSELL: But you were going to?

TAFT: Yes, of course. I was going to tell her. Her
Royal Highness is no fool, even if you might
like to think so. She'd have got your number
in half a minute. Come to think of it, Russell,
I'm not even sure if you're capable of seeing
it through. Perhaps we're asking too much of
you.

RUSSELL: The price is high, but I'm still interested.

TAFT: But can you do it? As you say yourself, you're
not born to it. It has to be in the blood.

RUSSELL: Colonel Taft, I shall do my best.

TAFT: Hm. Well, we've no choice. I'd better go and
break the news to Her Royal Highness. Have
some breakfast, learn your lines, study that
plan of the ceremony, and keep your mouth
shut in front of the servants. Come on,
Withers, you'd better come too. Oh, by the
way, the Princess is a very devout young
woman. You do believe in God, don't you?

RUSSELL: Not necessarily.

TAFT: Oh, well. She'll just have to believe for both
of you. At least try to look as though you
believed in that sword a bit.

(He and WITHERS *go out.* RUSSELL *mimes a
little with his sword, then gives up. He tries
kneeling and walking up the aisle. He prastises
a Royal Walk, a Royal handshake, a Royal
tour of a factory. He is just about to launch an*

51

ocean liner—"And may God bless all who sail in her"—when the FOOTMAN *and* TWO OTHERS *come back into the room with breakfast. They lay and prepare it, while he does his best to look nonchalant.)*

RUSSELL: *(finally).* That'll—*(regaining his vocal register)*—that'll do. Colonel Taft and Captain Withers will have theirs presently. I'll have mine now.

FOOTMAN: Very good, Your Royal Highness.
(The other two go out, and RUSSELL *sits down while he is served by the first* FOOTMAN.)*
Kidneys? *Your Royal Highness?*

RUSSELL: Yes, yes, yes. Please.
*(*RUSSELL *looks cautiously at the smiling* FOOTMAN *as he waits on him.)*
Er——

FOOTMAN: Yes, Your Royal Highness?

RUSSELL: Oh, nothing, nothing. That's all, thank you.
(Pause.)

RUSSELL: You can go now.

FOOTMAN: Very good, Your Royal Highness. Perhaps Your Royal Highness was thinking he had seen me before?

RUSSELL: Well, I——

FOOTMAN: You see, like Your Royal Highness, I'm here on my Press Card too.
(He bows out.)

RUSSELL: Oh, God!
(Finally, he shrugs and starts on his breakfast.)
Well—*(lifts up silver dish)*—*live* while it lasts!
(He starts to eat. As he does so a WOMAN *suddenly bursts in through the door. She closes it behind her sharply, leaning against it, panting lightly. She is scarcely forty, wears a macintosh,*

52

a plastic head cover and carries a large bag,
almost like a kit-bag.)

WOMAN: Oh!

RUSSELL: Who are *you*?

(*The* WOMAN *stares unbelievingly at him.*)

You! (*Grandly.*) What do you want?

WOMAN: Oh! Your *Highness*!

RUSSELL: Eh? You're not an assassin, are you? What
are you doing here? Eh? How did you get
into the Palace? You don't live here, surely?

WOMAN: Oh! Your Highness!

RUSSELL: Don't keep saying that. Where have you come
from? (*Pause.*) You do speak English, do you?
Where have you come from?

WOMAN: Well, I—I—Oh, Your Highness!

RUSSELL: Come over here. I'm trying to have my
breakfast. What do you want?

WOMAN: I've been in the laundry chute, you see, Your
Highness. Oh dear, I'm sure I look
such a mess!

(*She steps forward, and takes off her mac.,
hat, etc. Underneath, she is wearing a reasonably
smart, mass-produced dress with a quantity of
cheap jewellery. From her bag, she takes high-
heeled shoes, which she puts on, replacing the
galoshes she has been wearing. She takes a
sharp, distressed glance at herself in a hand
mirror.* RUSSELL *is intrigued, but goes on with
his breakfast.*)

RUSSELL: Why are you doing all that?

(*She ignores him, her concentration is so intense
for the moment.*)

Well—think I'll take off my sword.

(*He does so, placing it beside the dish of*

53

kidneys.)
What have you been doing in the laundry
chute? Is that why your dress is slightly
creased?

WOMAN: Oh! Is it? Where? Where? Show me! No,
you can't! Oh, dear! Oh, dear!
(RUSSELL *watches her, as, obsessed and
absorbed, she studies and rearranges herself.
He decides she's harmless, and, studying the
plan of the cathedral and the royal route, gets
on with eating his breakfast. Finally, the*
WOMAN *decides that there is no more she can
do about her appearance, and, after carefully
arranging her macintosh and bag on a chair,
she steps forward uncertainly.* RUSSELL *ignores
her. She coughs, putting all the gentility she can
make into it. There is no response, so she comes
a few steps downstage and repeats it.* RUSSELL
looks up.)

RUSSELL: You can't read a map, can you?

WOMAN: No, Your Highness, I'm afraid I can't actually
——

RUSSELL: No? Well, it's not so much a map as a
plan——

WOMAN: (*eagerly*). Oh! Is it a plan of the Royal Route?
I cut mine out of the papers days ago.

RUSSELL: Did you? Then perhaps you'd explain this
one to me.

WOMAN: Oh, really! May I?

RUSSELL: Sure.

WOMAN: *May* I? Your Highness?

RUSSELL: If you wouldn't mind——

WOMAN: Mind!

RUSSELL: You look a little bit odd. Are you all right?

54

WOMAN: Your Highness! I'm more all right at this
moment than I've ever been in my entire life!

RUSSELL: Perhaps you'd like a cup of coffee?
(*She nods.*)
Hang on.
(*He is just about to pour a cup, and then
hesitates.*)
I'll call the footman.

WOMAN: Oh, no! Don't do that!

RUSSELL: Why not?

WOMAN: Oh, don't do that, I beg of you, Your Highness,
don't give me away!

RUSSELL: Away?

WOMAN: Nobody knows I'm here——

RUSSELL: Ah, yes——

WOMAN: You don't know what I've been through for
this moment! How I've waited and waited,
and longed—and prayed to God and
thought——

RUSSELL: How long were you in the laundry chute?

WOMAN: Two days.

RUSSELL: What? Were you buried under the royal
laundry, I suppose?

WOMAN: Yes! (*Rapturously.*) For two whole days and
nights! But even that was wonderful. It was
worth all the planning and sacrifice, Your
Highness. I just lay there, breathing it
in, and, do you know, I could have stayed
there for ever. I felt a sense of peace and
contentment and well-being in that place,
under all your dirty clothes, like I've never
known in my life before.

RUSSELL: Would you like a brandy with your coffee?

WOMAN: Oh, thanks very much, Your Highness. Bit

early in the day for me—but, well, in the
circumstances——

RUSSELL: How did you know this was my room?

WOMAN: Oh, I know this place like the back of my
hand. I know where you all live and eat and
sleep, and . . .

RUSSELL: But, tell me, dirty laundry, as such, doesn't
have any special attraction for you?

WOMAN: Certainly not! There's nothing like that about
me. I'm a married woman——

RUSSELL: Children?

WOMAN: Three, Your Highness. Renee, that's my
eldest, she'll be seventeen next month, and
then Gloria, she's just fourteen. And the boy,
Anthony, he's eight.

RUSSELL: Yes?

WOMAN: Yes. He's the youngest.

RUSSELL: You mean the other two are older?

WOMAN: That's right, Your Highness.

RUSSELL: But does your husband know where you are?

WOMAN: Well, he doesn't know exactly where I am.
(*Giggles.*) He'd have a shock if he saw me
having a drop of brandy at this time of the
morning! He's not a drinker himself, you
see. . . . I mean he doesn't mind those who
do, but he never does himself. It has no appeal
to him.

RUSSELL: What does appeal to him?

WOMAN: Well, he's pretty keen on the football, and the
television quite often—though he won't watch
the plays. He'll go out of the room if I put a
play on.

RUSSELL: What's he doing now?

RUSSELL: What's he doing now?

56

WOMAN: Oh, he's minding the children.

RUSSELL: And he's quite happy to do that, is he?

WOMAN: He doesn't mind. He's used to it. He'll help
get them their teas when he's at home, and
when he's not, Renee's a very good girl, she
does it. His hours are a bit irregular. He's an
inspector on the buses, you see. So he's very
busy just now, what with all the crowds and
that.

RUSSELL: But he doesn't mind you going off, and dis-
appearing for a few days at a time?

WOMAN: Oh, my goodness, no! (*She laughs.*) Old Bill
doesn't care much about anything really. You
can't ruffle him, not even if you was to tell
him the world was coming to an end! Oh,
dear, Your Highness, I do hope you'll forgive
me, but I think your brandy's gone to my head
a bit——

RUSSELL: Have some more——

WOMAN: Oh, no——

RUSSELL: On the House—of Bamberg——

WOMAN: Oh, no, I couldn't, really——
(*He pours some.*)
Well, I suppose just a little drop then. After all,
it's a real occasion for me, this doesn't happen
to me every day. (*Passionately.*) Oh, Your
Highness!
(*She breaks off as though she might suddenly
cry.* RUSSELL *begins to look alarmed.*)

RUSSELL: Perhaps you ought to have some breakfast——

WOMAN: Yes, well you might be right! I haven't had
much for two days, apart from a few sardine
sandwiches and a tomato.

RUSSELL: You had those in the laundry chute?

57

WOMAN: Yes.

RUSSELL: (*helping her to breakfast*). Allow me.

WOMAN: Oh, no, I couldn't—please, you mustn't. Well, oh dear, well thank you, thank you very much. Yes, that'll do very nicely. Oh, kidneys! Oh, how nice! Oh, what a surprise! I feel as if I'm dreaming. (She giggles again.) But I'm not. I'm not dreaming, am I, Your Highness? It's real, all absolutely real. I'm sitting with the Prince, His Highness, in the palace, having bacon and eggs.

RUSSELL: And kidneys.

WOMAN: And kidneys! And brandy! Oh, I wish my friend could see me now. She'll never believe it.
(*She giggles again and drops a slice of bacon into her lap.*)
Oh, dear, now look what I've done! No, please don't get up, Your Highness. Please! It's my own fault. Oh dear, I am awful. It's that drop of brandy I expect. (*Suddenly very cross.*) Oh damn! All down my best dress!

RUSSELL: Have another.

WOMAN: I can't go out and buy one now.

RUSSELL: (*handing her another rasher and a drink*). Here.

WOMAN: Oh well, we only live once, as they say.

RUSSELL: That's right. It's a great day for both of us. Here's to it.

WOMAN: Cheers!

RUSSELL: Cheers!

WOMAN: (*in a soft whisper*). Your Highness.
(*They eat but the* WOMAN, *inflamed by the brandy, cannot take her eyes off him. Presently he begins to feel the strain.*)

RUSSELL: You don't think Bill's concerned about you?

58

WOMAN: (*wearily*). Oh, Bill——

RUSSELL: You don't think you ought to give him a ring?

WOMAN: No.

RUSSELL: I suppose he's used to your going off?

WOMAN: He just thinks I've taken up my usual place
outside the palace. That's my sleeping bag
I've got in there, you see.

RUSSELL: You seem quite well equipped.

WOMAN: And my little stove, and my transistor,
magazines and blankets, in case it gets a bit
chilly. Oh, I'm an old hand, Your Highness.
(*Suddenly almost collapsing with emotion.*) Oh,
Your Highness——

RUSSELL: (*staving her off*). But, tell me—just exactly
how did you get into the palace?

WOMAN: When I think of you——

RUSSELL: You must have been very determined.

WOMAN: You and your *bride*! (*She seems to put all the
emotion of her lifetime into the word "bride".*)

RUSSELL: Security must be pretty ropy.

WOMAN: Your *magnificent* bride!

RUSSELL: Do you think so?

WOMAN: Oh—*Your Highness.*
(*She stares at him with fierce sexual longing,
and her face begins to harden.*)

RUSSELL: You don't seem to be eating your kidneys.
Are they all right?

WOMAN: It's no good——

RUSSELL: Shall I send for some more?

WOMAN: I couldn't eat a thing.

RUSSELL: I'll ring for the footman——

WOMAN: No, don't do that! I can't do anything while
you're in the room.

RUSSELL: I think perhaps you ought to go. You're

looking——
(*She throws herself on to her knees and moans wildly.*)

WOMAN: Your Highness!
(*Horrified, he tries to help her to her feet, but she hurls herself at his boots in a rugby tackle.*)
No, no, you mustn't—please, Your Highness. I beg you, you mustn't. Your Highness, my Highness, forgive me! Forgive me! (*Ecstatically she kisses his polished boots.*)

RUSSELL: I forgive you all right. Now, why don't you——

WOMAN: Don't ridicule me.

RUSSELL: I'm not——

WOMAN: Don't ridicule me!

RUSSELL: I just——

WOMAN: I love you. You're all I ever think about. I love you. I am your most humble, I'm your most loving subject. I just love you. I worship you. I love you. You are my one and only god. Oh, Your Highness! Have a little pity.
(RUSSELL *looks down into her face, contorted with raw desire.*)

WOMAN: (*in a whisper*). You know what I want. You can see it, can't you?
(RUSSELL *nods.*)
I'm prepared to die for you. I mean it. Just for a few precious moments. Less.
(*There is an ugly challenge in her glance. And she leaps up and goes over to her bag.*)

WOMAN: All right, if you don't believe me—oh where is it? Damn! Just a minute—ah!
(*She brings out a large obsolete-looking pistol.*)

RUSSELL: What are you doing with that thing?

WOMAN: It's a souvenir. Bill took it off a dead officer

in the war.

RUSSELL: Well, put it away.

WOMAN: Oh no, Your Highness, my darling, my darling, my only real darling, I have to call you that. I couldn't shoot at you. That—that would be like trying to shoot at God. (*Hopelessly.*) You see?

RUSSELL: I do now.

WOMAN: Your Highness. . . .

(*Pause. She eyes him like a snake about to strike and advances slowly towards him.*)

If you don't . . . if you don't, if you don't, do what I, what I desire . . . (*she's said it now, so she repeats the word more hungrily than ever*) . . . what I desire more than anything else in this world—I shall turn this gun on myself, so help me God, I will——

RUSSELL: On your *self*?

WOMAN: Your Highness.

RUSSELL: Madam, I'm sorry but I must contain myself for my bride.

WOMAN: Oh God!

RUSSELL: Now, please put that thing away——

WOMAN: (*with triumph*). I knew you'd say that! I knew it in my heart of hearts. After all, what else could you say?

RUSSELL: What? About my bride?

WOMAN: Your Princess. Your magnificent Princess.

(RUSSELL *moves to her.*)

Keep away!

RUSSELL: But, please listen, Mrs.——

WOMAN: Mrs. Robbins.

RUSSELL: Mrs. Robbins.

WOMAN: I'm not fooling——

RUSSELL: Mrs. Robbins, now don't be silly.

WOMAN: This is my whole life—in a few moments——

RUSSELL: But it isn't. It can't be. Think of Bill, and Renee and Gloria and—the youngest.

WOMAN: (*calmer now*). Please, Your Highness; I ask you, do not mock me. We little people, who watch, and worship, and lead our little, unimportant lives, we have our little place, our little dignity. I ask for one thing.

RUSSELL: Anything.

WOMAN. A kiss.

(*He moves to her.*)

NO!

(*She goes to him as if she were the centre of some sacrificial procession, transfixed, like someone sleep walking. He puts out his cheek, she ignores it, takes his hand, kneels, and kisses it lingeringly.* RUSSELL *tries to make a grab at her pistol, but she is too alert. She leaps back.*)

Keep back!

RUSSELL: Put that away.

WOMAN: You're too late. You're much, much too late, but it was worth it. *It was worth it.*

(*Putting the pistol to her head she shoots herself, slumping on to* RUSSELL'S *foot. However, he manages to roll her off and grasps the nearest brandy. The* FOOTMAN *rushes in.*)

FOOTMAN: Phew! Who did it?

RUSSELL: What? She did, of course.

FOOTMAN: Who was she?

RUSSELL: How do I know?

FOOTMAN: Are these her things here?

RUSSELL: Yes. Her sleeping bag. And transistor. Here, you can't go through her things like that.

They're private.

FOOTMAN: Hm. Electricity bill and letter addressed to her. Mrs. William Robbins. Children?

RUSSELL: Three. Here——

(*Enter* TAFT *and* WITHERS.)

TAFT: What's going on? Good heavens! Is she dead?

FOOTMAN: Yes, sir.

RUSSELL: She shot herself.

TAFT: Lunatic, I suppose.

RUSSELL: No. just a loyal subject.

TAFT: Why did she shoot herself?

RUSSELL: She asked too much, too much from life and too much from me, in particular.

TAFT: Ah! (*To* FOOTMAN.) Here—you, take her outside, somewhere. Captain Withers will give you a hand.

WITHERS: Yes, sir.

TAFT: Only hurry. The Princess will be here in a minute.

(WITHERS *and the* FOOTMAN *collect up the* WOMAN'S *belongings, pile them on to her body and are about to carry her off.*)

RUSSELL: Just a moment. What's that footman's name?

TAFT: Name?

WITHERS: Robert, isn't it?

TAFT: Come along, Your Royal Highness, there isn't——

RUSSELL: His name isn't Robert and he knows I'm not His Highness.

(*The* FOOTMAN *stands holding one end of the* WOMAN'S *body. Then, his face breaks into a smirk.*)

TAFT: Is this true?

63

(The FOOTMAN *nods.)*

I see.

*(*COLONEL TAFT *takes out a small automatic and walks gravely towards the* FOOTMAN *whose smirk freezes into disbelief, the* WOMAN's *body slipping from his hands. He looks around for escape, but* WITHERS *is already blocking the doorway.)*

FOOTMAN: There's nothing you can do, you know. You can't get away with this. *(Appealing to* RUSSELL.*)* Russell—tell him——
*(*TAFT *shoots, and the* FOOTMAN *drops dead beside the* WOMAN.*)*

TAFT: Poor devil! Shifty face though.

WITHERS: He was fairly new, I think.

RUSSELL: He was a journalist.

WITHERS: Journalist! Good lord!

TAFT: Well, that's not so bad then, after all. Withers, you can tell Commodore Crabtree to issue a statement saying the woman shot him by mistake and then turned the gun on herself.
(Enter PRINCESS MELANIE. *She stares at the bodies.)*

MELANIE: Who are they?

TAFT: It's Robert, Your Royal Highness.

MELANIE: I can see that. It's that new, clumsy one.

TAFT: It seems, Ma'am, he was really a journalist.

MELANIE: Well, that explains one or two things. And the woman?

TAFT: Lunatic.

MELANIE: Well, can't you get rid of them or something?

TAFT: Withers!

WITHERS: Yes, sir.

RUSSELL: Here, shall I give you a hand?

64

MELANIE: Don't be ridiculous. Stay where you are.
(WITHERS *drags out the bodies.*)

WITHERS: It's all right, Your Royal Highness. I can manage.

MELANIE: And do close the door, for heaven's sake!

RUSSELL: (*weary and irritable by now*). You're not in a very pretty mood, are you?

MELANIE: The news is not exactly welcome—Mr. Russell.

RUSSELL: (*relenting immediately*). I'm sorry. Of course, you must be very upset.

MELANIE: Upset! Of course I'm upset! What stupid words you use. (*To* TAFT.) He's not very intelligent, is he?
(TAFT *shrugs, humbly and helplessly.*)

MELANIE: Still, neither was poor Willy, but I was very fond of him. The only time he ever put his foot down was in those absurd sports cars. Oh!
(*Her voice breaks, more with frustration than deep sorrow.*)

MELANIE: And—you!

TAFT: (*to* RUSSELL). Apart from breaking the tragic news to Her Highness, I've also done my best to outline the present situation, particularly as it affects the Constitution and the country as a whole. Unfortunately, personal grief for those in exalted places cannot be allowed to——

MELANIE: Oh, really, Taft—you are the most tiresome man in the entire world! Constitution and country! Do you think I don't know all that stuff backwards?

TAFT: (*persisting gravely*). Her country's honour must at all times take precedence over her

65

personal grief, however bitter, however tragic.

MELANIE: (*stamping her foot*). Taft! If you say that once more, I shall scream!

TAFT: I beg your pardon——

MELANIE: Oh, go away or something. I want to talk to this man. What's your name?

RUSSELL: Russell.

MELANIE: Russell.

TAFT: May I just remind you both of something very important. Time is short.

(*He goes out.*)

(*Pause.*)

RUSSELL: He's right. It's almost light already. And I still haven't learnt my lines.

MELANIE: Russell . . .

RUSSELL: Colonel Taft seems to think there's some Bamberg stuffed away in me somewhere.

MELANIE: I must say you look extraordinarily like poor Willy.

RUSSELL: Thanks.

MELANIE: You're not to make me cry. This is quite difficult enough as it is.

RUSSELL: Sorry.

MELANIE: There's something—something indefinably insolent about you.

RUSSELL: I don't know any better.

MELANIE: You'll have to start learning. Do sit down. What makes you think you can impersonate someone like Willy, anyway?

RUSSELL: What you said: insolence, I guess. Anyhow, you don't have to go along with the idea if you don't like it.

MELANIE: Oh, don't be ridiculous.

RUSSELL: Eh?

MELANIE: I have no choice.

RUSSELL: Duty?

MELANIE: Yes, I suppose you think that's very amusing. Why are *you* prepared to do it?

RUSSELL: For the loot.

MELANIE: Loot?

RUSSELL: Loot. Come on—you see home movies. I've read about it. You like musicals and light comedies.

MELANIE: Oh—money.

RUSSELL: Oh—money.

MELANIE: But do you mean you'll do anything for money? Anything?

RUSSELL: No, not anything.

MELANIE: What do you mean? And why do you have that weird accent?

RUSSELL: I've not had all that many offers. I might marry *you*, for instance——

MELANIE: Is it Australian?

RUSSELL: Yes. Mind you, that's for *real* loot.

MELANIE: Well, it's quite hideous.

RUSSELL: The loot?

MELANIE: No, your accent. You'll have to try and say as little as possible for the first few days. Or you can pretend it's one of his—your—tiresome jokes.

RUSSELL: I see. I make tiresome jokes, do I?

MELANIE: Constantly. Willy was just a schoolboy— everyone knew that. And don't say "loot" again. You're only doing it to irritate me.

RUSSELL: Am I?

MELANIE: Oh, do stop it.

RUSSELL: You know, I hadn't realized how sexy you are. You look to me as if you enjoy it.

67

(*She looks as though she might slap his face.
Or not.*)

Well, I shall be finding out soon enough—
shan't I?

(*But she decides to play it cool.*)

MELANIE: And you—you enjoy it, I suppose?

RUSSELL: Oh, yes. I'm not bad at it either.

MELANIE: You surprise me.

RUSSELL: I dare say that's the Bamberg in me.

MELANIE: I dare say. (*Suddenly lost.*) Well——

RUSSELL: I think I'm going to enjoy this job.

MELANIE: (*recovering*). You're a cheap little man, aren't
you?

RUSSELL: Yes. Very. But I'm all you've got.

MELANIE: I don't think you have any, any idea of what
you're in for.

RUSSELL: I've been making enquiries. And seeing you's
clinched it.

MELANIE: Don't try to be gracious. It's a little pathetic.

RUSSELL: I'm not being gracious. It's the truth. Being
alone with you in this soft, grey light, being
so close to you, I suddenly understand the
meaning of royalty. I feel the long, thrusting,
sexual stimulus of the crown.

(*For a few moments they simply look at each
other in the cool light.*)

MELANIE: (*softly*). Do you know what to do?

RUSSELL: I think so.

MELANIE: I mean—during the ceremony.

RUSSELL: I'll manage.

MELANIE: I tell you: you don't know, you simply don't
know what you're letting yourself in for.
You've no idea of what it's like.

RUSSELL: I'll risk it.

68

MELANIE: You'll be like a badly trained poodle going through its odious little tricks for the rest of your life.

RUSSELL: I told you: you've sold me on it.

MELANIE: But you don't know what it's like. Some days your head will start to spin with boredom.

RUSSELL: Like yours.

MELANIE: Like mine. But I'm used to it. I've been trained to it. But you—you'll crumble and disintegrate with boredom. Your blood will rush with constant hot and cold running boredom.

RUSSELL: Do you know: there's still a little spark of life left somewhere there in you. I can see it, I can actually see it now. Somewhere, there's a little blundering glimmer of life left in you.

MELANIE: My whole weary system is spinning around forever like a royal satellite in a space of infinite and enduring boredom. Oh, my God, I am so bored! (*She goes to the window.*) I am so bored, do you hear me, my people? My countrymen, I am so bored, and most of all, I am bored with you, my people, my loyal subjects, I am so bored that even this cheap little Australian looks like relieving it for a few brief moments, now and then, in the rest of my lifetime.

RUSSELL: Just a few moments.

MELANIE: Very well.
(*They gaze at each other again.*)

RUSSELL: (*presently*). Looks like we've got a deal.

MELANIE: Yes. (*Pause.*) Do you want to kiss me?
(*He does so. She begins struggling, and pushes him away so that he falls to the floor. She looks*

69

disturbed and frightened.)
I can't bear to be touched!
(She goes out. Enter TAFT.*)*
RUSSELL: See you in church.

CURTAIN

End of Scene 1

ACT TWO

Scene 2

The Cathedral. Fanfares. Salute of guns. Pealing bells. choir of splendid voices. All the massed devices of a Bamberg occasion, in fact. MELANIE *and* RUSSELL *are kneeling before the altar and about to get up and begin their slow procession. Standing solemnly in the front choir stalls are the Bamberg Family.*

Downstage, WIMPLE *and five other journalists are poised, waiting to describe the scene.* WIMPLE *we know. The* FIRST JOURNALIST *is a weary, solemn fellow from a weary, solemn newspaper. The* SECOND JOURNALIST *is a bright, eager lady from a retarded glossy. The* THIRD JOURNALIST *is from a right, rasping popular daily. The* FOURTH JOURNALIST *(lady or gentleman, it doesn't matter) is from a mass woman's weekly. The* FIFTH JOURNALIST *is the correspondent of a large American News Agency.*

TAFT *and* WITHERS *stand to attention in full dress uniform nearby. But before* WIMPLE *can start wimpling, the* ARCH-BISHOP *speaks before the altar.*

ARCHBISHOP:

> Lord, make us instruments of Thy will; where
> there is hate, may we bring love; where there
> is offence, may we bring pardon; where there is
> discord, may we bring peace; where there is

71

error, may we bring truth; where there is doubt, may we bring faith; where there is despair, may we bring hope; where there is darkness, may we bring light; where there is sadness, may we bring joy. O Master, make us seek not so much to be consoled as to console; to be understood as to understand; to be loved as to love. For it is in giving that we receive; in self-forgetfulness that we find; in pardoning that we are pardoned; in dying that we shall wake to life eternal; where Thou livest and reignest in the glory of the blessed Trinity, one God, world without end.

WIMPLE: (*scarcely breathing*). Now—as the royal couple, still kneeling on their faldstools, bow their heads before the Archbishop, the choir and congregation sing the cheerful and intensely singable hymn, personally chosen by the couple themselves, "O Perfect Love". In just a moment, with the final triumphant fanfare, sounded by trumpeters from the Prince's own regiment, the Royal Bamberger Blues, you will see the Prince and his bride slowly move along the aisle to the Great West Door. My goodness, what a uniquely impressive sight it all is! The Gentlemen-at-Arms are there—you can probably see them—impassive as always, the plumes of their helmets moving . . . just ever so slightly in the merest current of occasional air. If this were to be the end of all, I think we could bravely—yes, bravely—say that it was a good and a glorious end. Over there, on the right, and next to His Majesty, is the young Prince Henry, looking more confident than

72

when we saw him last on a similar occasion, the wedding of his aunt last year. A fine, handsome young man in his uniform, looking as cool as —as a cucumber. From left to right, you can see, or should be able to see, Princess Mariana, Duke George Stettin-Bamberg, the head of the Stettin-Bambergs, Princess Theresa, the Grand Duchess Isabella, Her Majesty the Queen, the young Prince Henry, His Majesty the King . . . Ah . . . now, they are, yes, they are beginning to rise—oh, what a moment, what a moment as the bride's train fans out in a fantastic, iridescent light, her veil, a superb cloud of zephyr-light silk tulle floats away there effortlessly, right there to the full extent of her exquisite train. Oh, oh, it's quite unbelievable in its solemn beauty, this moment. . . . In loose formation, behind her, walk the pages and bridesmaids—including Princess Mariana. . . . Now—Princess Melanie is indeed one of the family, and, as her handsome soldier husband leads her down the aisle, her royal cousins look on approvingly. What a sight it is! What a happy day for everyone! Only a very crabbed and gloomy heart could look on at this superb and moving spectacle without pride in his bosom and a catch at the back of his throat. (WIMPLE *has a discreet catch at the back of his throat, while the other* JOURNALISTS *take over.*)

FIRST J.: It is all extremely picturesque, in the highest Bamberg tradition, measured and somewhat reminiscent of a Fackeltantz, which, it may be recalled, is a dance with torches in which only members of the blood royal may take part.

73

SECOND J.: The King looks especially handsome today in the full dress ceremonial uniform of the Twelfth Bamberg Lancers, with full decorations, of course. . . .

THIRD J.: As one looked at her, the joy seemed almost too much for her slender figure to contain. But, as she was about to leave the altar, her face flew asunder in a great, glowing smile of simple, unaffected happiness.

FOURTH J.: Beautiful wasn't the word for this bride. She was perfection. Against the greatest competition in the world, she moved like the right, royal lady she is. Like some serene swan, she floated rather than walked, down the aisle with her handsome soldier husband, towards her place in history.

FIFTH J.: It is perhaps difficult for Americans to fully comprehend the strange, remote, religious element of majesty in these high European occasions. However, there is certainly no denying the extraordinary appeal of it, and ever since the first royal limousine, with its transparent hood, set out on the route, there has been fantastic frenzy here, in this ancient city that makes a New York City ticker tape parade look like a high town carnival. No one yet knows the number of men, women and children trampled to death in the mass enthusiasm, or even those who have perished from exposure. However, it is believed that the figures are considerable, and the casualty stations—socialized, of course—have been working at top pressure for hours.

(*The swelling volume of majestic sound and*

74

sense of hysteria becomes more and more intense and claustrophobic. The JOURNALISTS *have to raise their voices a little, but they rasp on mechanically, lifelessly.*)

FIRST J.: The Royal Wedding unites two families which both trace their ancestry in direct succession to King Stephen the First. Prince Wilhelm shares with Princess Melanie a

> great great great
> great great great
> great great great
> great great great
> great great great
> great great great
> great-grandfather. However, in the

case of the Princess, the number is one less.

SECOND J.: The Queen, lovely as always, is wearing a Marshall Waters powder blue ribbed satin outfit, with Saint Cyr hat in lilac organza. (*The Prince and Princess are making their way down the aisle to the front of the stage.*)

FIRST J.: Happy is that land where the desire for symbols and display is expressed so harmlessly and yet so richly. Truly, an orb in the minster is worth a monster in orbit.

THIRD J.: To see this proud, fragile, yet superb rose of womanhood is almost too much for description. One can only try. Humbly and thankfully.

SECOND J.: Princess Theresa, always a treasure in pale colours, is wearing a frost-like satin outfit made by Percy Cummins. . . .

FOURTH J.: I think this has been the most romantic Royal Wedding of them all. Once or twice, the Prince seemed nervous and unsure of his lines, even fumbling some of the time-honoured gestures. But the Princess, by his side, quietly helped him through, and the few hold ups that there were seemed scarcely noticeable. . . .

SECOND J.: The Grand Duchess Isabella is wearing a Cummins Champagne-coloured silk organdie outfit, embroidered with gold, diamanté and topaz.

FIFTH J.: It may be mysterious, incomprehensible but it's moving, certainly most important of all, it's moving. And a vindication of the Western Way of Life, against the threat of the Communist world. In all of this, my friends, our bastion lies.

FOURTH J.: Yes, I think the moment I shall cherish most of all from this thrilling day is when the Princess looked up at her soldier husband, and smiled reassuringly at him, during the solemn service. It was an unforgettable moment, and, do you know, from where I was sitting, I suddenly saw her radiant young face look up into his and—yes—she *winked.*

SECOND J.: Isabella is in deep azalea organdie, fashioned by the House of Clough. . . .

FOURTH J.: She winked. . . .

(RUSSELL *and* MELANIE *stop downstage.*)

RUSSELL: (*smiling royally*). I should have brought my camera.

MELANIE: No more pictures!

TAFT: (*to* WITHERS). He's a Bamberg all right.

WIMPLE: And now, ladies and gentlemen, our National Anthem!

(ALL *stand to attention.*)

Long live the Bambergs

76

God Save Our Noble House
Long Live the Bambergs
Bless Our Noble House
Our Loving Prince and Princess
Our Kings and Noble Queens—
Long live our god-like—Kings and
    Queens!

CURTAIN

End of Play

Number Two

UNDER PLAIN COVER

A Play in One Act

CAST

    ·

TIM
JENNY
POSTMAN
STANLEY
WEDDING GUESTS
REPORTERS

UNDER PLAIN COVER

The outline of a house. Facing the audience a front door.
Then, centre stage, a living room leading on to a bedroom.
Beyond that a small room. All that can be seen of the
bedroom is the bed, or part of it, through the partially open
door.

In the living room there stands a dressmakers' dummy.
A surgical trolley, a couch, some sheets and blankets.

A postman carrying several parcels comes to the front
door and rings the bell. From behind the screen a young man
appears. He is dressed in a white coat with a stethoscope
round his neck. He is pulling his trousers on. His name is
TIM. *He calls to the bedroom.*

TIM: Will you go, or shall I?
   (*A girl's voice answers. It is* JENNY.)
JENNY: You!
TIM: I don't think I can. I've still got all this stuff
   on.
JENNY: Well, take it off. Damn it—it's not a full
   dress uniform.
   (*Bell rings again.*)
TIM: Damn! Please—you go. I went last time.
JENNY: Well, I should think so. I could hardly have
   gone in the circumstances. (*Giggles.*)
   (*He laughs too.*)
TIM: No, I suppose you couldn't really. Well,

83

I'm still clearing this stuff away.

(TIM *goes to the bedroom.*)

Be a good girl. Go on. You look all right. He won't notice.

JENNY: What do you mean—he won't notice. He can hardly help notice! Anyway, *who'll* notice?

TIM: The postman, you idiot. Come on. He's going away. We'll miss him.

JENNY: The postman. Oh, good. Are you sure?

TIM: Of course! (*Concerned.*) Darling—please. He's going away.

JENNY: Oh, all right then—I don't know what he'll think.

TIM: It doesn't matter what he thinks. He probably won't even recognize you.

JENNY: Of course he'll recognize me, you fool!

TIM: Answer the door!

(*He goes to the window and shouts out.*)

Just a minute. Please, darling!

(JENNY *appears. She is dressed as a housemaid.*)

JENNY: You don't think he'll think I'm the maid, do you?

TIM: (*agonized, pushes her*). Oh, never mind. Who cares! It might be for you.

JENNY: Oh, yes! It might come today. How marvellous.

TIM: Just a minute.

(*He grabs the green screen and takes it into the bedroom.*)

JENNY: (*calling out*). Coming!

TIM: All right. You know how prying people are.

(*She nods and goes to the door.*)

JENNY: Good morning!

POSTMAN: (*drily*). Thought you'd gone on your holidays.

JENNY: Sorry.

POSTMAN: One for you. One for *Mr.* Turner.
(*He gives her a receipt to sign.*)

JENNY: Here?

POSTMAN: Usual place. Like one long Christmas for you, isn't it?

JENNY: (*coldly*). Thank you.

POSTMAN: Well, if it weren't for people like you and Mr. Turner I suppose there'd be no work for people like——

JENNY: No. Good morning.

POSTMAN: Cheerio!
(*She closes the door, examines the parcels.*)

JENNY: Darling!

TIM: (*off*). Did he notice anything?

JENNY: They've come.

TIM: Oh, good!

JENNY: I don't think so. He was a bit cheeky, that's all. He's not as nice as the other one. Well, he'll get nothing at Christmas.

TIM: He must have thought you were mad. Must think I'm mad too to let you do it.
(TIM *enters from bedroom. He is dressed in striped trousers and black jacket. He carries a copy of* Country Life *and* The Lancet.)
That's them! Isn't that super!

JENNY: There's yours. Shall we open them now?

TIM: No, let's keep them for later.

JENNY: Oh, come on—I'm dying to open them.

TIM: Well, that's fine. All the better. It'll do you good to wait.

JENNY: I don't want to wait.

85

TIM: Well, you've got to.

JENNY: Why?

TIM: Because *I* say so.

JENNY: Pooh!

(*His manner slides into a silky, menacing, authoritative tone, slightly upper class. She becomes pert, cheeky.*)

TIM: Hand me those parcels!

JENNY: What for?

TIM: Never mind what for—just hand them to me, and don't be impertinent.

(*She hands them to him.*)

JENNY: What are you going to do with them?

TIM: They're going into the staff room.

JENNY: Boo! I want mine!

TIM: You'll have it all right.

JENNY: When?

TIM: Later.

JENNY: Want it now.

TIM: You'll get it now, but you'll get something else.

JENNY: What will I get?

TIM: Wait and see.

JENNY: What will I get?

TIM: No.

JENNY: Go on.

TIM: No. Get my tea and tomato sandwiches.

JENNY: Please.

TIM: You heard me.

JENNY: Please—sir.

TIM: That's better. Well, Jenny, when you've got my tea and tomato sandwiches, we may discuss your problems then.

JENNY: Now!

86

TIM: (*anxiously*). I think you mean it.

JENNY: I do.

TIM: (*in more ordinary voice*). Do you?

(*She nods smugly.*)

Aren't you tired?

(*She shakes her head.*)

Blimey—well, you're a stronger man than I am. I need a cup of tea first, after that last lot.

(*She moves towards the bedroom.*)

TIM: NO!

(*She faces him mockingly. He resumes character.*)

Jenny! if you do not serve tea in—precisely two minutes——

JENNY: But I can't.

TIM: You'll have to.

JENNY: But it's not possible.

TIM: Everything is possible.

JENNY: No—it isn't. That's what you always say.

TIM: (*coaxing*). And aren't I right?

JENNY: No.

TIM: Jenny, serve tea. At once!

JENNY: What happens if I don't?

TIM: Do you really want to know?

JENNY: Yes. I think so.

TIM: If you don't serve my tea and tomato sandwiches—and everything must be absolutely immaculate, mind. Just as if it were a really posh house and you had to do this every day.

JENNY: Every day!

TIM: *You* should complain! The whole thing must be beautifully done. *You* know.

JENNY: Oh!

TIM: What?

JENNY: I don't think there are any clean napkins!

TIM: (*grimly*). There'd better be.

JENNY: Oh dear!

TIM: Or there'll be trouble.

JENNY: What sort of trouble?

TIM: Big trouble.

JENNY: How big?

TIM: Enormous.

JENNY: Well, go on—how big is that?

TIM: More than you can cope with anyway, young lady.

JENNY: (*mocking*). Oh, you're frightening me to death.

TIM: Now then!

JENNY: Sir!

TIM: Any more talk like that and you could find yourself in serious trouble. And you don't want that, do you?

JENNY: Oh, no, sir.

TIM: That's right.

JENNY: I've always been a very careful girl, sir.

TIM: Not careful enough.

JENNY: What's that?

TIM: Don't say what's that to me, girl. What do you call me, when you address me?

JENNY: Sir.

TIM: And what do you do?

(*She curtsies. Does it badly and giggles.*)

JENNY: That wasn't very good.

TIM: No, it wasn't. I'll let it pass this time, but watch it.

JENNY: Yes, sir.

TIM: Watch it, because I've got my eyes on you
all the time.

JENNY: I know, sir.

TIM: Every little move you make. Every little
tiny slip goes down as a mark against you.

JENNY: A mark, sir?

TIM: A black mark.

JENNY: Oh dear, sir. Have I got any black marks
already?

TIM: You have.

JENNY: How many?

TIM: (*smugly*). Quite a few.

JENNY: But how many, sir.

TIM: You'll find out.

JENNY: But I want to know, sir.

TIM: (*cruelly*). Why?

JENNY: Well, if I don't know, I may get upset and
worried about it, when I'm getting the tea
ready, and——

TIM: Yes?

JENNY: I may not serve it properly.

TIM: (*with crushing coolness*). Well, that's *your*
little problem isn't it. Now, don't stand
around here talking all day. Serve tea.

JENNY: Yes, sir.

TIM: My lord.

JENNY: Yes, my lord. Oh—are you a lord?

TIM: Yes, I think so. Let's try it and see.

JENNY: All right. I don't think it's so good, though.

TIM: Why?

JENNY: I don't know. I don't think you look quite
right in that.

TIM: Yes—maybe you're right. O.K. Leave it as
it was. (*Reverting to character*.) Go on then.

You don't want your cards, do you?

JENNY: No, sir.

TIM: You don't want to be dismissed without a reference, do you?

JENNY: Oh no, sir.

TIM: Think how upset your family would be if you lost your job. What would your father do to you?

JENNY: Take off his strap to me, sir.

TIM: Yes. There are plenty of girls just waiting, longing to step into your shoes.

JENNY: Yes, sir. Oh—is this the nineteen thirties?

TIM: Yes.

JENNY: When did you think of that?

TIM: When do you think? Just now.

JENNY: Oh, what a good idea! Oh, please, sir. I need the job badly. Dad's still on the dole, and both me brothers are down bad.

TIM: Well, then—you'd better watch your behaviour, hadn't you?

JENNY: Yes, sir. I will. I'll do anything you say, sir —Anything.

TIM: Very well then.

JENNY: Just give me a chance, then.

TIM: Now don't get hysterical, my dear. You'll be all right so long as you do exactly as you're told.

JENNY: Really, sir?

(*He nods, benignly.*)

Then I can stay, sir?

TIM: For the moment, Jenny, you may stay. And if I am satisfied with you, you may have no fears.

JENNY: Oh, thank you, sir.

TIM: That's enough. Tea, Jenny!

JENNY: Yes, sir. At once, sir.

TIM: Quickly, quickly!

JENNY: Oh, I'll try and not make any mistakes, sir. I'll do everything just as you like it, sir.

TIM: All right, but I'll be watching you, Jenny. Remember, I'll be watching you.
(*He goes and sits down to read* Country Life. *She goes to the kitchen unit. Presently.*)

TIM: I'm waiting. (*Pause.*) I am waiting for my tea! (*Bawls.*) JENNY!

JENNY: The bell!

TIM: What? Oh, yes.
(*He rings a sash bell.* JENNY *"appears".*)

JENNY: Yes, sir?

TIM: The tea, Jenny. Where is the tea?

JENNY: I'm sorry, sir.

TIM: Don't stand there saying you're sorry.

JENNY: I'm sorry, sir.

TIM: Oh, for heaven's sake, girl, don't whine. I can't stand it. What's the delay? Um?

JENNY: Well, I've got to wait for the water to boil.

TIM: Wait for the——! Jenny, are you being impertinent?

JENNY: No, sir—I——

TIM: I asked you a question: are you being impertinent?

JENNY: I'm sorry, sir. I'm not feeling very well.

TIM: I've told you: don't snivel. You make me sick, people like you. Do you think someone like me is interested in your squalid little problems?

JENNY: No, sir—only——

TIM: Now, what is it? I warn you, Jenny. I am

really beginning to lose my temper.

JENNY: Oh, no——

TIM: And you know what that's likely to mean,
don't you?

JENNY: Oh, no—please, sir!

TIM: Well—you haven't much time.

JENNY: Excuse me, sir—the kettle's boiling, sir.
(*Goes to make tea.*)

TIM: (*quietly*). My patience is beginning to run
out.

JENNY: Coming, sir! Just a few minutes.

TIM: Too long!

JENNY! What's that, sir?

TIM: I say too long. A few minutes is too long
for a man like me. One minute.

JENNY: Oh, sir——

TIM: One minute.

JENNY: Two minutes, sir. You'll have it in two
minutes.

TIM: One minute!

JENNY: One minute!

TIM: One minute!

JENNY: Make it two, please, sir.

TIM: One.

JENNY: It isn't long enough.

TIM: It's all you've got.

JENNY: Oh! (*Wails.*) How long have I got now,
sir?

TIM: One minute, beginning now——

JENNY: Just a minute!

TIM: What?

JENNY: Where's the flipping tea trolley?

TIM: In the bloody bedroom—where else?

JENNY: Oh, sorry.

92

TIM: Twit. A right bloody housemaid you'd make.

JENNY: All right, don't go raving mad. I forgot.

TIM: Yes, you forgot, didn't you! You forget too bloody much. Just you wait. One minute— from now.

JENNY: (*cheeky, her identity poised*). Well, you do look cross.

TIM: Ten——

JENNY: You don't look very grand and sophisticated, do you?

TIM: Twenty——

JENNY: If I were a housemaid——

TIM: *What* did you say?

JENNY: Sorry. Well, you didn't look as though you'd command much respect from a dumb little tart like me.

TIM: Thirty——

JENNY: Oh, that's better. I say, you look quite terrifying now——

TIM: Forty——

JENNY: No, stop counting—that's not fair.

TIM: Forty-five——

JENNY: Oh, hell. I don't know what I've done with the bread and butter now.

TIM: Too bad. Just what I fancy today. Fifty——

JENNY: Oh, dear. Oh, there it is.

TIM: Brown, of course.

JENNY: Phew! Thank God I remembered.

TIM: And some white. Fifty-five.

JENNY: White!

(*She grabs some and puts it on the trolley.*)

TIM: I hope you haven't forgotten anything. Sixty! You know how important my tea is to me. If I don't have it just as I like it, exactly as I think about it, it makes me unhappy, and I feel lost and lonely. You're ten seconds late. And then I get vicious because even the tiny indispensable comforts of life are being denied me. And I need comfort, I need the comfort of home-made jam. Apricot jam. Twenty seconds late.

JENNY: No!

TIM: Blackcurrant jam and rhubarb jam that my father used to eat when he was a boy, and I've never been able to find or persuade anyone to make. Thirty seconds.

JENNY: It's here! It's here, sir. Here it is, sir. Your tea, sir.

TIM: And bloater paste and hot buttered toast. And gentleman's relish. Forty seconds.

JENNY: No—not forty seconds! It's here. Tea is served, sir.

TIM: And radishes! Hard and crisp and sparkling. Where are the radishes?

JENNY: On the little plate, sir.

TIM: Where?

JENNY: There, sir.

TIM: They don't look like the kind of radishes I always used to have. They're frozen radishes.

JENNY: No, sir.

TIM: How dare you, miss.

JENNY: No, sir—picked out of the garden, sir.

TIM: Frozen radishes! Fro—Radishes!

JENNY: No, fresh, sir.

TIM: Don't lie to me. You were one minute late in serving tea.

JENNY: No, sir—one minute.

TIM: One minute!

JENNY: Forty seconds, sir.

TIM: Fifty seconds.

JENNY: Forty, sir.

TIM: Fifty.

(*She is about to argue. But he quells her.*)
Ah! Now then, do you know what happens to naughty little housemaids who bring me my tea late.

JENNY: No, sir.

TIM: Don't you?

JENNY: No, sir.

TIM: Well, for every ten seconds that they're late——

JENNY: Every *ten* seconds!

TIM: Every ten seconds.

JENNY: It was thirty last time.

TIM: Never mind. It's ten now. You've been very naughty.

JENNY: Well, it's not fair.

TIM: Of course, it isn't fair. As I was saying, for every ten seconds that you are late, you will be very severely punished.

JENNY: Every ten. That's four.

TIM: Five. Very severely indeed.

JENNY: You seem to make up all the rules.

TIM: Naturally. That is what I was born to.

JENNY: Well, I think I'll give in my notice.

TIM: You can't.

JENNY: My dad'll understand—especially when I tell him the kind of man you are. I'll get another job.

TIM: It's the nineteen thirties.

JENNY: Oh yes, I forgot that.

TIM: Well, you haven't much choice, have you?

JENNY: I suppose I haven't.

TIM: Speak up. And pour me my tea.

JENNY. Yes, sir.

TIM: In addition to this other punishment, you have a considerable number of black marks against you.

JENNY: Oh! Have I? Many?

TIM: About a dozen.

JENNY: A dozen! There can't be.

TIM: You've just put sugar in my tea. That's thirteen.

JENNY: Oh!

TIM: There's no jam spoon, fourteen; cake knife, fifteen, and I can see a slug on the watercress—*two* black marks for that! That's seventeen altogether, and I've hardly begun.

JENNY: Oh, sir, it's too much!

TIM: Whose fault is that?

JENNY: I'll try, sir, honestly I will!

TIM: You should have thought of that before, shouldn't you!

JENNY: I don't think I can bear it!

TIM: You've got to.

JENNY: Have a little mercy, sir.

TIM: You must learn to take your punishment properly.

JENNY: I'm an ignorant girl, sir!

TIM: So much the better!

(*She starts snivelling.*)

Stop that! You'll have something to snivel for later. Go and wait for me.

JENNY: No, sir.

TIM: JENNY!

96

JENNY: Very good, sir.

TIM: Well, what are you waiting for?

JENNY: How many did you say, sir?

TIM: Seventeen.

JENNY: Seventeen!

TIM: Plus five.

JENNY: Plus five. Oh—I'd forgotten that.

TIM: Yes. I thought you might have. Get along then.

JENNY: How long will you be?

TIM: Sir?

JENNY: Sir.

TIM: I don't know how long I shall be, Jenny. I shall see. But I shall certainly finish my tea first.

JENNY: But you don't know what it's like to wait!

TIM: I—don't know—what it's like—TO WAIT!

JENNY: Forgive me.

TIM: You shall wait even longer. Just for that.

JENNY: Well, not too long then, because I'm——

TIM: You've already got seventeen plus five. You don't want any more, do you?

JENNY: I've gone.

(She disappears into the bedroom. He settles down rather agitated to his tea.)

TIM: Ugh! You do make a lousy cup of tea.

JENNY: *(off)*. What's that?

TIM: I'm damned glad I don't employ you, that's all.

JENNY: Can't hear you.

(Pause. He eats.)

TIM: No tomato sandwiches.

JENNY: What you say?

TIM: No tomato sandwiches.

97

JENNY: Oh, my God! I forgot.

TIM: You forgot all right. Well, you're in dead trouble now!

(*He munches over* Country Life.)

JENNY: (*off*). I'm ready.

(*He ignores her.*)

I said—— Yoo hoo! I'm ready!

TIM: What is that to me, girl? Domestic servants do not shout through open doors at their masters.

JENNY: Please—I'm sorry, sir.

TIM: No excuses. That's even more trouble.

JENNY: No.

(*Pause.*)

Please. I'm exhausted.

TIM: Well, that's just too bad. You bloody wait!

JENNY: (*off*). What?

TIM: I said you bloody wait, you horrible little skivvy!

JENNY: Oh!

(*Whimper off.*)

TIM: (*settling down*). I'm having my tea.

FADE

Downstage a reporter appears. He is middle-aged and the worse for wear.

REPORTER: Just an ordinary, young married couple you might think. A lot of people are inclined to sneer at us, but in my job you do get to know quite a bit about human nature and what makes people tick. Their hopes, and fears, their little ambitions. Take this couple

98

for instance: not long married, not too well off, but doing quite nicely, both working till they decide to start a family. Like a million others. Or, at least, that's what they thought. That's what you would have thought—ordinary members of the public. That's what I would have thought.

(*The* POSTMAN *crosses to the front door.*)

REPORTER: Excuse me——

POSTMAN: Yes?

REPORTER: Are you delivering that at this house?

POSTMAN: I am.

REPORTER: Mr. and Mrs. Turner, isn't it?

POSTMAN: That's right. What do you want?

REPORTER: What sort of couple are they?

POSTMAN: Just an ordinary couple. Here, you're Press, aren't you?

REPORTER: Don't tell me *you've* got a grudge. We did you boys rather well over your wage demand, didn't we?

POSTMAN: (*drily*). Thanks, mate. You can carry me sack for me, too, if you like.

(*Goes to door, rings, whistles. Lights up in house.* TIM *is reading the mail order advertisements in a pile of newspapers. Occasionally he marks one. He is dressed as a boxer in bright shorts, dressing-gown, boots and gloves. Over by the screen is a milliner's dummy wearing a corset.*)

TIM: Darling!

JENNY: (*off*). If you mean the door bell, I'm not answering it.

TIM: Why not?

JENNY: Don't be so dim!

TIM: Well, I can't go. He'll go away again. Oh, do go!

(JENNY *appears. She is dressed as a Girl Guide.*)

JENNY: I can't go like this.

TIM: Yes, you can.

JENNY: Well, I won't.

TIM: You can pretend you're someone else. That hat just about covers your face.

JENNY: Go on!

TIM: How can I go? With these. (*Lifts his gloves.*) I can't even open the door handle. I'm helpless.

JENNY: I'll say you are! Oh, all right then. They can wait a minute.

(*He puts the dummy behind the screen.*)

TIM: (*calls out*). Coming!

(*He nods to her and sits down.* JENNY *opens the door.*)

JENNY: Good morning!

POSTMAN: Thought you'd fallen down the hole.

JENNY: What hole?

POSTMAN: One for Mrs. Turner.

(*He gives her the receipt to sign.*)

JENNY: Here?

POSTMAN: That's right. Mrs. Turner away?

JENNY: Yes.

POSTMAN: Who are you? You're the little sister, I suppose.

JENNY: That's right. Nothing for Mr. Turner?

POSTMAN: No. That's all this time.

TIM: Oh, *hell*!

POSTMAN: Cheerio then!

JENNY: 'Bye!

100

(*She closes the door.*)
What a shame!

TIM: Damn!

JENNY: Never mind.

TIM: I'd been thinking about that all the morning.

JENNY: Perhaps it'll come this afternoon. Look—mine's come.

TIM: Well, that's something.

JENNY: Well, that's something. Don't be such a misery. Or I shan't open it.
(*She goes into the bedroom.*)

TIM: Where are you going?

JENNY: (*off*). To take these off.

TIM: Oh! Aren't you going to open it?

JENNY: I don't know.

TIM: What do you mean, you don't know?
(JENNY *appears at the door, taking off her tunic.*)

JENNY: Depends how you are.

TIM: Here, help me off with these gloves, will you?

JENNY: (*going into bedroom*). Hang on for a bit, I want to hang this up before it gets creased any more.

TIM: Whose fault is that?

JENNY: I don't know what you mean. I feel rather good today.

TIM: Yes. I think I do too. I liked this morning.

JENNY: Well—(*parody*)—it's something different.

TIM: Yes. Makes a change.

JENNY: Bit more out of the usual run, like. What's in the papers?

TIM: I haven't had a chance yet. I wish you'd help me with these gloves. I'm breaking my

101

teeth on these strings.

JENNY: Don't be so impatient.

TIM: Hey, what are champers?

JENNY: What are what?

TIM: Champers.

JENNY: Spell it!

TIM: C-H-A-M-P-E-R-S.

JENNY: Never heard of them.

TIM: Oh—I see!

JENNY: They sound a bit exotic.

TIM: It's all right. It's champagne.

JENNY: You fool!

TIM: It's the way I read it. Only it looked a bit sort of medieval in the context. Like he died of a surfeit of champers. Did I tell you about the Champagne Queen?

JENNY: No—what?

TIM: He likes to get his boy friend's slipper— and drink——

JENNY: Don't tell me——

TIM: Oh yes, and then there's the Jessie Matthews Queen.

JENNY: What about her?

TIM: She dances overhead, on the ceiling, on my bed! Help me!

JENNY: Coming!

(*She comes in wearing a dressing-gown, helps him off with his gloves.*)

TIM: And then we can look at your parcel.

JENNY: Papers first.

TIM: Usual stuff, I think.

JENNY: Never mind. We don't want to miss anything.

TIM: There's a picture of George and Betty's

wedding in the local.

JENNY: Oh, where? Let me see.

(*Shows her.*)

They look nice. I'm crazy about that dress. Why don't we get one?

TIM: What a smashing idea. Where?

JENNY: I don't know. Expensive item. That's why we got married in a registry office, remember?

TIM: When? When can we have——

JENNY: You be a good boy. And we'll see.

TIM: Jenny——

(*He kisses her.*)

JENNY: Yes?

TIM: Please can we have a wedding dress like Betty's?

JENNY: We'll see.

TIM: Perhaps we could have Betty's. People don't want wedding dresses after they're married.

JENNY: We'll see.

TIM: Oh, you sound like my bloody aunt.

JENNY: I'll give you a good smack in a minute.

TIM: You didn't say that when I had the gloves on.

JENNY: Looks a super wedding. Wish we'd gone.

TIM: Well, I don't.

JENNY: I think we ought to go out sometimes.

TIM: You don't really want to go out, do you?

JENNY: No, not really. Only——

TIM: Only what?

JENNY: No, you're right. I don't really want to either. Anyway, you'd have had to be the Best Man.

TIM: I thought of that. Might have felt a bit

103

funny, standing up there at the altar. You know—when you've been on intimate terms with the bride *and* the groom. Who's that?

JENNY: Which?

TIM: The bridesmaid—second from the right.

JENNY: That? Oh, you know who that is—that's Brenda.

TIM: Brenda——

JENNY: Brenda Rose.

TIM: Brenda Rose. Of course, I remember her— years ago. Tall.

JENNY: That's right.

TIM: I remember her very well. She had very fair coloured hair, and deep blue knickers.

JENNY: That reminds me——

TIM: What?

JENNY: Papers.

TIM: All right. Papers. Then parcel. Right?

JENNY: O.K.

(*They settle down happily, seriously.*)

TIM: She was a funny girl.

JENNY: Who?

TIM: Betty.

JENNY: Oh!

TIM: Rather toffee-nosed sort of girl. Always used to take her dog with her to parties so that she could talk to it—just to show how bored she was.

JENNY: Sounds sweet. Here, is this the same as ours?

(*Hands him paper.*)

TIM: (*reading*). "Adjustable Dress Dummy. In tough plastic. Thirty-eight shillings." How

104

much was ours?

JENNY: You know, I can't remember.

TIM: "Fully finished set of parts which clip together and adjust to size and height. Can grow and change with you."

JENNY: Oh, yes, that must be it.

TIM: "No skill, tools or extras required. Money back guarantee."

JENNY: Well, I wouldn't mind having ours back.

TIM: No, it was a bit of a washout, that, wasn't it?

JENNY: Hey, do men get a funny feeling when they do their coat buttons up?

TIM: What—overcoat?

JENNY: Well—yes.

TIM: Don't know. Can't say I've noticed it. Why? Do you?

JENNY: Yes.

TIM: How interesting. Do all women?

JENNY: Shouldn't think so.

TIM: You've never mentioned that before.

JENNY: I suddenly realized it yesterday morning when I took my coat off at the office. I thought of you.

TIM: Darling. "Wendle's Specialist Commode five pounds twelve and sixpence. Made by craftsmen with real oak finish. Upholstered seat covered with green simulated leather. Hygienic pan with handle."

JENNY: I've got one here for only four pounds ten, delightfully discreet. This has a hygienic polythene pan. Can't you forget your rupture?

TIM: Don't.

JENNY: This is the modern method of control, gentle, natural, easy.

TIM: It will enable you to carry on your normal pursuits, however strenuous, without under-straps, hip pressure or chafing.

JENNY: You can experience for the first time a real feeling of elation.

TIM: Hooray! ! Hallo, hallo. There's a plastic object here. As used by the Convent of St. Bridget in Limerick. It has a little battery in it that lights up.

JENNY: Maternity fashions.

TIM: Oh, yes—read those.

JENNY: Thought that would rouse you. Um . . . oh, it's not very interesting.

TIM: Come on. Read it out.

JENNY: No really. It's just rather dull, really. . . . Nothing for us.

TIM: I wish you wouldn't keep staring at my hairline.

JENNY: Was I?

TIM: Yes, you make me feel I've got dandruff.

JENNY: Sorry.

TIM: Well, don't look away like that. You've been transfixed above my eyeline for ten minutes.

JENNY: I haven't.

TIM: Well, have I?

JENNY: What?

TIM: Got dandruff?

JENNY: Oh, don't be silly——

TIM: Have I?

JENNY: Yes.

TIM: Oh, God, I knew it! Damn you!

JENNY: French rubber gloves.
(*Goes to mirror.*)
TIM: Damn! So I have.
JENNY: Ah! Here it is! "Sensational value!
Directoire knickers."
TIM: Yes.
JENNY: "Three pairs for fourteen and eleven. Hips
thirty-eight to forty-four."
TIM: Gosh, why do they make them so bloody
big?
JENNY: Always the same. "Three pairs for seventeen
and eleven. Hips forty-six to fifty-four."
TIM: Forty-six to fifty-four!
JENNY: Good night! "Made in wonderful heavy
quality interlock. Long leg——"
TIM: Darling——
JENNY: Yes? "And wide gusset."
TIM: Do you think I'm fixated?
JENNY: No, I don't think you are.
TIM: Are you sure?
JENNY: Why? You don't think you are, do you?
TIM: No, I'm quite sure I'm not. I just wondered
if you thought so.
JENNY: No. I'd tell you if I thought so.
TIM: Let's have some coffee. I feel tired.
JENNY: I'm not surprised.
(*She goes to the kitchen unit.*)
And then we'll open our parcel, shall we?
TIM: O.K. (*Sings.*)
Knickers, knickers, these are the thing
to 'ave,
You puts them on in the bedroom,
You takes them off in the lav——
JENNY: Are you all right?

107

TIM: Yes, I'm all right.

Knickers, knickers, these are the things
to wear,
For if you buy a pair of knickers,
Then you won't have your bum all bare.
Why? Don't I sound all right?

JENNY: No, you sound a bit depressed.

TIM: Oh, sorry.

JENNY: That's all right.

TIM: Well, I am a bit. Hey—do you think we're
living on relics?

JENNY: Who?

TIM: You and me.

JENNY: Probably.

TIM: So do I. Do you think they're diminishing
in some way?

JENNY: What?

TIM: Well, knickers, for instance.

JENNY: No, why should they be?

TIM: You're sure?

JENNY: Quite. Why, aren't you?

TIM: I think so. I ask myself: *am* I diminished?
But I can't always be sure.

JENNY: You brood too much. You should get out.

TIM: I don't want to get out.

JENNY: All right. Well, maybe sometimes you
should, anyway.

TIM: What do they represent, in particular?

JENNY: Take down your particulars.

TIM: Your step-ins.

JENNY: Your what?

TIM: I seem to remember that once. Your
drawers, your taxi-teasers, your unmen-
tionables. What do we know about them?

108

Are they symbols then? In that case, not only do they convey ideas, but they do things. Saint Augustine once said that a handshake doesn't just express friendship. It promotes it. Your milk's boiling over.

JENNY: Damn! Go on!

(*She rushes to milk.*)

TIM: Or is it straightforward and not really open to serious speculation? Like my hairdresser said about that new musical in London; no message, dear. Just lots of lovely people enjoying themselves. Do we demand an ethic of frankness? Or is it simply a matter of private faces in public places? But should the facts about recusant lingerie be made known? Are they to be pressed in old books and forgotten, instead of being tended as objects rooted in the deepest needs of the personality. Attention must be paid!

JENNY: Hear, hear!

TIM: Great love spring from great knowledge.

JENNY: We've got that——

TIM: This is the most challenging moral issue of our time.

JENNY: The choice between open ends and E.T.B.s.

TIM: Elastic top and bottoms. Oh, I've just thought of another—The Judas Queen.

JENNY: What does she like?

TIM: Being picked up in a loo, and then betrayed to the police. Oh, you'll wonder where the fellow went, when they wash your brains in Pepsodent.

JENNY. Here's your coffee. You sound a bit better.

TIM: Just a little.

JENNY: Why don't you take off your dressing-gown?

TIM: Why?

JENNY: You look hot.

TIM: I am hot. I've always been hot. When I was younger I was skinny and afraid to take my clothes off. Now I'm ashamed because I'm too fat.

JENNY: You're not too fat. I think you're just right.

TIM: Well—I'm twenty-nine. Not much time. Erasmus didn't start learning Greek till he was thirty-four, you know. Still, there's a lot of difference between him and me. Oh, thou that tellest glad tidings to Zion, arise, shine, for thy light is come.

JENNY: Have you got sugar?

TIM: No—fattening. Get thee up into the high mountain! Why don't we have another baby?

JENNY: Why not?

TIM: That's good. I wonder if Erasmus wore knickers.

JENNY: He probably didn't think they were important—very significant.

TIM. Probably. You won't forget about getting that wedding dress, will you?

JENNY. No.

TIM: Promise?

JENNY: Promise.

TIM: Only if you get pregnant again, we shall need it.

JENNY: Don't worry. I'll get it.

TIM: Hey, you know that woman in the hospital.

JENNY: The Lady Almoner?

TIM: That's right—the one who——

110

JENNY: The one you say looks just like me.

TIM: Yes.

JENNY: Charming.

TIM: Give us a kiss.

JENNY: What about her?

TIM: Give us a kiss!

JENNY: Oh, all right.

TIM: Why don't you——

JENNY: Why don't I get an overall just like hers!

TIM: That's right. Well?

JENNY: I've already thought of it. We've been spending far too much lately, you know that.

TIM: Oh, come on—you look just like her.

JENNY: No!

TIM: All right—you don't look like her.

JENNY: Well, we'll see.

TIM: What about her? The Lady Almoner?

JENNY: What—underwear?

TIM: Yes. Pretty meagre I should think, wouldn't you? Sort of shrivelled, crabbed, paltry things.

JENNY: Oh, absolutely. Ungenerous. Nothing expensive or friendly or welcoming.

TIM: Exactly. Nothing comforting or reassuring. Oh, God: isn't it a mess!

JENNY: Yes.

TIM: The Vision of Knickers that thou dost see, is my Vision's Greatest Enemy.

JENNY: Who said that?

TIM: Blake.

JENNY: Yes, I thought it was. As a matter of fact, I can tell you exactly what they'd be like.

TIM: What?

JENNY: The Lady Almoner's.

TIM: Oh yes?

JENNY: Well, in the first place, white, I should say.

TIM: Oh yes—white definitely.

JENNY: Upper class colour—they nearly always wear white. With a slip always. And the satin ribbon a little too loose. Pants with what are called French ends—open ends in the trade. Er. Wearing *cornet du bal*.

TIM: Yes. Absoutely. Perfect. I was wrong. You're not like her at all.
(*Kisses her.*)

JENNY: Do you think there are many people like us?

TIM: No. Probably none at all, I expect.

JENNY: Oh, there must be some.

TIM: Well, yes, but probably not two together.

JENNY: You mean just one on their own?

TIM: Yes.

JENNY: How awful. We are lucky.

TIM: I know.

JENNY: What's the matter?

TIM: I don't know. I think I feel ill.

JENNY: In what way?

TIM: Every way. I'm always feeling ill, and there's nothing at all the matter with me. Isn't it boring. I wish I wasn't so boring.

JENNY: You're not.

TIM: Well, I wish I wasn't feeling ill anyway.

JENNY: Still?

TIM: No. I'm slightly better.

JENNY: If I open the parcel—will that make you feel better?

TIM: I don't know. Wait for a few minutes. Maybe if I have another cup of coffee I'll

112

feel better. I wanted to ask you something.

JENNY: Yes?

TIM: What was it? Oh, yes—I have an *idée fixe*——

JENNY: Oh, no you haven't. I wouldn't have one in the house.

TIM: Really. I know. Tell me, I want your definition.

JENNY: You don't remember it very well. I've explained it to you enough times.

TIM: Well, I like to hear you say it. Go on.

JENNY: Oh, all right——

TIM: Oh, just a minute—I've thought of something.

JENNY: Well?

TIM: The Prime Minister's Country House—Seat: Knickers.

JENNY: Of course. Why don't you come down for the week-end?

TIM: Open to the public on weekdays.

JENNY: Until they pull it down. Well now——

TIM: Oh, yes—remind me to tell you something afterwards.

JENNY: Shall I begin?

TIM: Please. Oh, just while I remember: it is *interlock* we don't like, isn't it?

JENNY: Yes. Now.

TIM: Sorry. Why did the lady with a wooden leg have no change for a pound?

JENNY: Oh, all right, if——

TIM: She only had a half a knicker.

JENNY: (*firmly*). First of all—pants. To a specialist, one should remember that this is not the generic word. It means that they don't have

113

elastic at the bottom.

TIM: Just left open to speculation.

JENNY: Exactly. The Americans have perverted this, and created a very loose generic word "panties". Now, briefs are what every girl wears nowadays.

TIM: Alas!

JENNY: Closed at the bottom of the leg, and leaving about four inches of girdle showing on the thigh. Then there are what are called bikini briefs.

TIM: And very nasty too!

JENNY: Which are the final sophistication of the brief form, and leave the navel showing as long as you haven't a girdle on. And about, oh, six to eight inches of flank. Finally we come to the flower of the form, believed by most to be decadent. They have long legs, never more than about four inches above the knee, which makes sitting down, getting out of cars, riding bicycles or going upstairs in buses a tremendous adventure. They always—repeat always—have elastic top and bottom. What the flying buttress was to Gothic so is elastic top and bottom to the Classical Perpendicular or Directoire style. And it is only in knickers that one is still able to find that strange repository of mystery—the gusset.

TIM: Ah—the gusset—I wonder what that chap Betjeman would say about all this.

JENNY: Nowadays they are mostly worn by elderly or very square middle-aged ladies, and can still be bought in fast decreasing numbers from places like Debenham and Freebody, although High Street Kensington still remains the richest field, with Derry and Toms and, above all, Pontings, stubbornly carrying on the old tradition. I suppose one might almost say that the end of the knickers came with the rise of nylon.

TIM: True. It was nylon really killed them.

JENNY: They were never quite the same afterwards. The heavy whisper of descending pink silk was soon to be heard in the land no more. All was hard-faced, unembarrassed, unwelcoming nylon. Of course, in their most basic form, they can still be seen on schoolgirls trooping by the dozen into their gymnasiums in drab navy. But only very square little girls still really wear them long.

TIM: Yes, I remember them. Hundreds of them. Sometimes they were dark green.

JENNY: Bottle.

TIM: But mostly navy. Still, even they were better than nothing. They often had pockets in them, didn't they?

JENNY: That's right. I used to keep my handkerchief or toffees in there.

TIM: Really? I once knew a girl who used to keep her sweet coupons in there. Then there were French knickers——

JENNY: And cami-knickers. They were very odd. I think my mother had them in her trousseau. It was really a truncated slip in what was known as art silk——

TIM: Like art cinema——

JENNY: It wasn't really silk at all. There was a

tongue at the front and the back of the
skirt which buttoned up in the crutch.

TIM: Or crotch as the case might be. What about
bloomers?

JENNY: I suppose they were really the first dab at
the form.

TIM: Mrs. Bloomer, that's right.

JENNY: Then I seem to remember there was something called a lingerie set, in one-faced satin,
which, I think, was dull on one side and
shiny on the other.

TIM: I adore listening to you talk.

JENNY: No, wait a minute—I'm wrong. They were
called a slip and knicker set. That's right.
You'd say: My mother's bought me a slip
and knicker set for Christmas.

TIM: You seem to know everything!

JENNY: Well, I'm going to open my parcel.

TIM: Oh, good.

JENNY: And you can change too.

TIM: Yes, I'd better, hadn't I?

JENNY: Yes, you had, or you'll get into trouble,
won't you. You look better after that.

TIM: Yes. I am. Thank you.
(*He goes to behind screen, to change.* JENNY
goes into the bedroom.)

TIM: Oh, I know what I meant to tell you. When
I was getting a postal order for that last
lot, I thought of a collective name for them.

JENNY: What, like a flock of knickers? Or a pride
of knickers.

TIM: Oh, that's not bad either. Mine's a charisma
of knickers.

JENNY: Too fancy.

116

TIM: (*disappointed*). Oh!

JENNY: Nobody knows what it means.

TIM: (*to himself*). Knickers, the eponymous hero of the trilogy. Hey, what about the critics?

JENNY: What about them?

TIM: Well, you know. This week, we have been to see knickers. What did we feel about this? *Soaptender:* Well, in the first place, there seemed to me to be far too much production. And production of a kind I find particularly irksome. After all, we *saw* all this in the twenties surely. Expressionism and everything.

JENNY: (*off*). If only the verse could be allowed to speak for itself.

TIM: Exactly.
(*He comes out dressed in winceyette pyjamas and heavy woollen dressing-gown.*)

TIM: As for the garment itself. Well, construction is weak of course. So is plot. But we have learned in recent years to bear with that somewhat in exchange for a little vitality. But somehow this elastic doesn't seem to know exactly what it's aimed at, and the final gesture is totally inadequate, irrelevant and with a basic failure to be coherent. We are left to work out our own causes. Futility is our only clue. It seems to me that these knickers are speaking out of a private, obsessional world—full of meaning for them. But has it any significance for us? I think not. On the whole, a dull, rather distasteful evening.

JENNY: Not without quality. On the other hand, I

117

would not say straight out it had no quality at all. What do the others think?

TIM: Doesn't seem to have found an entirely satisfactory form for what they are trying to say. The reason for the elastic is never clearly or adequately explained.

JENNY: By no means a total artistic success.

TIM: I thought them schoolgirlish and sniggering. Very tiresome indeed. At least bikinis are brief! It's all very vigorous in an undisciplined way. One does get so tired of these chips on the gusset. Very self indulgent and over-strident, especially in the length of leg, I thought. Colour was reasonable, but surely Herbert Farjeon did these with much more taste and economy?

And after all, this frenetic destructiveness is hardly helpful. What do they really offer to put up as an alternative? We are left unsatisfied with questions posed and nothing answered.

Hear, hear! This sour soufflé certainly failed to rise for me. Although everyone tried hard enough. I suppose what they were aiming at was pure lingerie. Ah—you mean like pure cinema. Exactly, and then, of course, there's the obvious influence of Genet. Indeed. To say nothing of:

James
Ionesco
Fanny Burney.

Troise

—and his mandoliers too. Let's not forget them. That influence is quite clear.

118

JENNY: How would you describe the style?

TIM: Style.

Florid
Decadent
Unnecessary repetition.
Neo-classical
Baroque
Kafkaesque
Fin de Siècle
Je M'en Fus
Arcane
Elliptical Elastical.

JENNY: So, how would you sum up, ladies and gentlemen?

TIM: Well, within their own terms, these knickers may seem to work, but what is the manufacturers' attitude to them?

JENNY: (*off*). What does "within their own terms these knickers may seem to work" mean?

TIM: It means you enjoyed yourself at the time, but now you're ashamed to admit it!
(JENNY *comes in dressed as a nurse in black stockings, standard cap and cuffs, etc.* TIM *whistles.*)

JENNY: (*brisk*). Come along, Mr. Turner, that's quite enough jokes for today. You know what we've got to do, don't you?

TIM: (*humbly*). Yes, nurse.

JENNY: Well, then, hurry up. Don't keep me waiting.

TIM: Sorry, nurse.

JENNY: You don't want me to get cross with you, do you. You're not feeling very strong either, are you, Mr. Turner.

TIM: No, nurse.

119

JENNY: Right, then. Let's watch ourselves and do exactly what we're told.

TIM: Yes, nurse. I will.

JENNY: Otherwise the consequences for you could be pretty nasty.

TIM: Promise, nurse.

JENNY: Into bed then. Sharp. Who's taken their rubber sheet off the bed?

TIM: I——

JENNY: You know what the rules are. Right! I'll remember that. What are you sniggering at?

TIM: Lord Knickers.

JENNY: What about him?

TIM: Family motto: Free to Bend.

JENNY: That's enough of your little jokes, Mr. Turner. I'm afraid I'm going to lose my temper with you.

TIM: No! No!

(JENNY *grimly wheels over the surgical trolley, rolls on gloves, and puts the screen round him. They both disappear behind it.*)

JENNY: Now!

(*The sound of struggling, then a mounting, muffled yell. A baby starts screaming.*)

JENNY: (*behind screen*). Damn!

TIM: (*behind screen*). Is that ours?

JENNY: Of course it's ours. You stay there.

(*She goes to the bedroom and reappears, holding baby in her arms.*)

TIM: Can I come out?

JENNY: No!

TIM: Please.

JENNY: No, I said!

TIM: I want a drink of water.

120

JENNY: You heard what I said. I don't want any naughtiness. You'll do as you're told. Like always.

FADE

REPORTER: Who would have thought least of all that ordinary, happy young couple with their everyday cares and worries, their two bonny babies, that destiny was about to strike them such a cruel, and horrifying blow?

As they sat in their little suburban home, watching the telly, planning for the kiddies' future, discussing the new light that needed putting in the bathroom—all the homely concerns of young people in love, how were they to know. How could they have known. They were innocent. And yet they were guilty. Guilty in the eyes of men and God. Yet, who could not wring pity from their heart at the hand Fate had played them. (*Less rhetorical, more saloon-bar style now.*) But this astonishing, human story really began for me on the Friday night I went into what we called the paper's branch office to have a drink before going home. Ned, the news editor, was there with his "school" all happily gathered round him, like a lot of little chicks round a hen. (*Settling down to be important.*) There are always similar "schools" in Fleet Street, and they usually form round some executive by men who think that diamonds may drop down one day from the

121

copy on his desk. I always liked Ned, and I respected him—I considered him to be a magnificent journalist and news editor. But I was never a member of his "school". I think I'll have another one—yes, double. I was probably a bit too successful for Ned's liking.

At that time I was very successful indeed. Yes, and that didn't really endear me. That's what the game's like. Fleet Street loves a failure, and I certainly wasn't a failure then. Why, if you take the trouble—I suppose you'd think it a bore wouldn't you? You're a bit bloody grand, aren't you? You think I can't afford to pay for a round of drinks, don't you! Well, you're bloody right, I can't. But if you had the ordinary human interest to look through the paper's files during those six years you'd see I had twice the space, twice the success, and twice the number of front page stories, more than any other member of the staff. What was I saying? Oh, yes. Little Jenny Turner. Well, now. On the Friday night then, I gave my usual friendly nod to Ned and everyone, and ordered a small beer. I was standing at the bar, thinking. I think a lot when I'm drinking. I don't suppose you'd believe it, but I do. Well, presently the 'phone rings and Ned has his ear to it for about ten minutes. Suddenly, he beckons me over, and he says: "Off you go, Stan. Just your stuff. In Leicester, there's a happily married couple with two children. Name of Turner.

Some clerk in the local Ministry of National
Insurance has just tipped us off."
(*Pause. He drinks, struggles to remember.*)
"It seems they're really brother and sister.
Call at the cashier's and I'll give you a chit.
If you get a move on you might get there
before they find out themselves. Best thing,
Stanley, would be if you could break the
news to them yourself." So that's how I
found myself in a suburban street in
Leicester on a cold February night. The
wind was howling away when I arrived.
(*Fade up on. House.* TIM *is sitting in the
living-room. He is wearing a black leather
motor cycling outfit. Very sharp. Beside him
is a cradle with a young baby in it. He is
nursing another. In the room are all kinds
of children's things: clothes drying on a horse,
toys, rattles, etc.*

TIM: Are you all right?
JENNY: Just coming.
TIM: Gosh, I do like the week-end.
JENNY: I know.
TIM: Don't be too long. I'm getting hot in this.
STANLEY: Tim seemed a nice, well-spoken boy. Quite
well up in things for a boy of his back-
ground, I thought. He seemed to be
something of an all-round athlete. Boxer—
keen motor cyclist. Even took an interest
in medicine, he told me. It was a pitiful
sight that little, untidy room with the
kiddies' things all over it. But they were
happy. They looked proud then, they could
still lift their heads up high.

123

(JENNY *comes in wearing a very elaborate wedding dress. She looks pregnant.*)

JENNY: Well?

TIM: (*breathtaken*). Marvellous. You look marvellous.

JENNY: What about the roses?

TIM: Super.

JENNY: Pink. Knicker pink. Plastic, I'm afraid.

TIM: Darling! It's marvellous.

JENNY: Wait till you see the rest.

TIM: I don't feel dressed properly.

JENNY: Never mind. We'll think of something.

TIM: Let's put the babies to bed. Shall we?

JENNY: Let's! Quickly!

STANLEY: It fell to me to break in on their simple happiness, and smash their dream world to smithereens. I didn't relish it, I can tell you. (*He rings the front door bell.*)

TIM: Who the devil's that?

JENNY: Damn!

TIM: (*calls out*). Who is it?

REPORTER: My name is Williams. Stanley Williams.

TIM: What do you want?

STANLEY: Is that Mr. Turner?

TIM: Yes.

STANLEY: I wonder if I could have a few words with you and your wife?

(TIM *and* JENNY *look at each other, baffled.*)

TIM: I suppose we'll have to let him in. Here—take the baby, will you?

JENNY: Just a minute.

(*She lifts up her wedding dress and pulls down her pregnant padding.*)

O.K.

124

(*She takes the baby.* TIM *opens the door.*)

REPORTER: Good evening. I'm sorry to bother you,
but—oh!
(*He stares at* JENNY *in her wedding dress and
the baby.*)
Mrs. Turner?

JENNY: Yes.

REPORTER: Oh, my God!

JENNY: What's the matter with him?

REPORTER: Forgive me. It was a shock. May I . . . may
I sit down for a moment?
(JENNY *kicks the padding out of sight.* TIM
shows him to a chair.)
Thank you, thank—— Well, I can tell you
life has dealt me some bad hands in my
time but—I'm sorry, but you don't have a
drink, do you?

FADE

(*The dark figure of* TIM *is sitting sadly in the
living-room.* STANLEY, JENNY, *and the two
children leave through a window. As they do
so, the* POSTMAN *is at the front door, haggling
with the reporters and cameramen over the
price for the exclusive right to the story.*
STAN, *looking wary and paternal, ushers*
JENNY *and the children downstage,* L., *with
him. He carries a suitcase and one of the
babies for her.*)

STANLEY: I was glad to get out of that one I can tell
you. What sickened me was the way every-
one behaved. As if it were a cattle auction.
I tell you, I could have cheerfully seized

125

hold of him and broken his neck. Cringing, pleading, whining. It was disgusting. (*To* JENNY.) You go round the corner, my dear, and wait in my car. They won't know you're gone.

(*She nods, takes the other baby, and moves a few paces downstage.* STANLEY *goes gravely over to the haggling group at the door.*)

POSTMAN: Hello, I've been expecting you. Well, now everybody's here, we can really get down to business. I've got the girl, and I've got the babies.

REPORTER 1: What about the husband?

POSTMAN: He doesn't matter. He's a bit mental, if you ask me. I'll tell you now, straight out. I'm out to get the highest price I can. I'm strictly a business man.

STANLEY: Nonsense. You're a postman.

POSTMAN: The paper that bids the highest will get the story, that's all.

STANLEY: (*righteously*). What do you think this is? A cattle market?

POSTMAN: All right—what's your bid, mate?

(STANLEY *hesitates. trying to look dignified. The other reporters make three-figure offers.*)

REPORTER 1: If you'll just wait half an hour until I can speak to my editor and get his O.K., I'll double all these bids!

POSTMAN: (*to* STANLEY). What's your bid?

REPORTER 2: I'll pay more than him!

REPORTER 3: How about two hundred quid, now, straight down in cash?

REPORTER 4: Will you take a cheque?

REPORTER 3: See, there it is. I've got it in my hand.

POSTMAN: All right then. Come on, *you*! I know you can afford it. Make your bid, then, or have you got to ask your boss first?

STANLEY: No, I don't. I'll make my bid now. Nothing! (*He summons himself up to a great moral occasion.*) And do you know why? Because I don't believe in all this trading in human beings. (*He begins to stalk away, and the haggling begins again. A reporter buttonholes him.*)

REPORTER: O.K. Stanley. But just to cover me can I tell my office how much you paid for it? Can I say you've given one thousand pounds? They won't go higher than five. Just to cover me.

STANLEY: You can tell your office I got it for free. (REPORTER *shrugs and moves off.* STANLEY *goes over to* JENNY *and takes the baby.*) Listen, Jenny, I'm not going to promise you any money, but right now I'll take you and your babies out of this place, into a decent hotel room where you can have a nice warm bath and a meal. And then when you feel better we'll talk. What do you say, Jenny? (JENNY *looks blank.*) She smiled through her tears and nodded.

JENNY: What about Tim?

STANLEY: He'll be all right. He won't leave that house. To be honest with you, Jenny, he seems to have a rather morbid obsession with the place, especially your possessions. It's understandable, I suppose—all the little things you'd bought together. He did want to come with you at first, but I talked him

127

out of that.

(*Away from her again.*)

Poor lad, he was so stunned, he couldn't see right from wrong at first. Well, I 'phoned the office and I said I can give you the exclusive story of the girl who married her brother, signed by her. I think you'll want to use it on page one.

Drop banner with Headline—

I MARRIED MY BROTHER

They did.

JENNY: I am the girl who married her brother. Yes, the handsome man who is the father of my two darling baby boys is my father's child, my mother's son. Now that the tragic truth is out I have decided to tell my full story— if only because it might prevent such a terrible thing happening again to anyone. It is the story of years of happiness as man and wife. And it ends with the most terrible day of my life—the day, four months ago, when we realized that we were the son and daughter of the same mother and father. As all the world knows by now, my brother, Timothy, and I were parted as children by our mother's death. He went into a home, and I was adopted by a Leicester couple.

I am still young. My life is before me. But I know that my future must not, cannot, include the man I love. Because the man I love is my brother.

STANLEY: I should have read her palm for her then. On the evening of the day that story was published, I introduced her to a young post

128

office clerk. Two weeks later they were
married.

(*He leads* JENNY *and the children off.*)

FADE

(*Wedding group with* JENNY *as the bride in
white.*)

STANLEY: Well, Jenny asked to go to London, where
she could lose her tragedy among the
hundreds which London bears in her great
heart every day. And sure enough she did—
only too soon. I liked her choice. He seemed
an admirably upstanding young man.
Frankly, I certainly preferred him to Turner,
who seemed a bit of an odd fish to me.
There was something solid about this other
boy, both feet on the ground. And, of
course, nothing wrong or perverted—in the
way the other relationship had been I mean.
(*During all this the happy group is being
doused with rice, photographed, etc.*)
My first reaction was to talk them out of it.
I felt it might not be wise for two young
people who had known each other such a
short time to join themselves in Holy
Matrimony. Especially as the young man
was so respectable. I returned to the office
and made my views known to the editor.
He didn't agree with me. He said most
impatiently, that if Jenny and this boy were
in love and wanted to marry it was none of
my business. What was my business, he was
most explicit to point out was to ensure that

129

if they did marry, our paper should have the
story of their wedding—with pictures—
exclusively. It was a tough assignment.
However, I was used to that. He gave me
authority to pay the expenses of the wedding,
to organize it, and to buy a trousseau for
Jenny second to none. Oddly enough this
aspect of it seemed to fascinate her more than
even the wedding itself. We spent days in
lingerie shops. Anyway, the big day came
round. Jenny was married with due solemnity
—it was a specially moving occasion for all
—and I was the best man. At the request of
the groom, I thought that was rather nice
of him.
(*A wedding reception is quickly improvised.*)
Jenny looked very lovely, I thought. Very
beautiful and radiant indeed, with an
enormous bouquet of pink roses. It's
occasions like this that make my sort of job
really worth doing. I arranged a slap-up
reception, managed to dodge the other papers
and everyone was happy. But I reckoned
without my editor. The wedding of the girl
who married her brother was too big to let
pass like this. Well, I suppose people want to
dig down so they can understand a little more.
(*Raises champagne glass.*)
To the happy couple.

BRIDEGROOM'S MOTHER:
Oh, it is lovely, isn't it. We are grateful, you
know. We'd never have been able to afford
anything like this.

STANLEY: It's a pleasure, my dear. A pleasure to see

130

such charming, delightful people blessed
with such good fortune.

BRIDE'S MOTHER:
You will try and keep this out of the other
papers, won't you, Mr. Williams?

STANLEY: Don't you worry, it's all being taken care of.
(*A reporter and a photographer approach.*
STANLEY *looks anxious.*)
Have some more champagne, my dear, with
the paper's compliments.
What are you two doing here?

REPORTER: Hello, Stanley. Seems we're on the same
story.

STANLEY: What do you mean?

REPORTER: I've got Turner here.

STANLEY: Who?

REPORTER: The brother, Tim. The brother.

STANLEY: Sh! Where is he?

REPORTER: Outside in the car.

STANLEY: What's the angle?

REPORTER: The loneliest man in Britain watches
wedding on the outskirts of the crowd.

STANLEY: Listen, I don't know what you're up to, but
I've promised these people a serious nice
wedding—not a peep show. And I'm keeping
to that.

REPORTER: Well, it's a good twist.

STANLEY: Damn your twist!

REPORTER: Relax, Stanley. You're drunk. You only try
to be moral when you're drunk.

STANLEY: These are nice people, and this is a solemn
and important day of their lives. I won't
have it made into a stunt.

REPORTER: Listen, Stanley, our instructions are to get

131

a picture of him congratulating the bride
and bridegroom.

STANLEY: But it's not possible. It just can't be done.
The young couple might allow it, perhaps
—though I'm not so sure. But what about
Mum and Dad?

REPORTER: That's your problem, Stanley. Remember,
we're waiting.

(STANLEY *sweats. The bridegroom's father
concludes a speech.*)

FATHER: And in conclusion, I should like to express
our deep, heartfelt gratitude to the man who
made all this possible, a good and loyal
friend—Mr. Stanley Williams.

STANLEY: (*rises and raises glass*). Ladies and Gentlemen,

Now, I have a very special toast to give.
I want us to drink to a man who has
suffered a great sorrow, a good, kind man,
who must be feeling very lonely today. The
older ones among us here, who watch the
happiness of this wonderful young couple,
do know that fate plays many strange tricks
on men and women as they make their
winding journey through life.

And the older folks here, I do know,
would want me to make this toast, just to
show, that in the hearts of none of us here,
lingers the slightest ill-feeling or hostility
to the lonely man who, though he is not in
our presence, must surely have been today
in all our minds. Ladies, and gentlemen, I
give you a toast to the brother of this lovely
bride—to Timothy Turner.

132

GROOM: To Timothy Turner.
      (*All drink.*)
ALL: To Timothy Turner.
GROOM: What a wonderful thought.
GROOM'S MOTHER:
      To her brother. We certainly bear him no
      ill-will. . . . To Timothy Turner.
ALL: To Timothy Turner.
JENNY: To my brother, Tim.
      (*A pause.* STANLEY *sweats and signals to a
      waiter to refill the glasses.*)
STANLEY: It is indeed a great pity that the brother of
      the bride is not with us here today. I am
      certain that all of us here would have been
      willing to let him share a little of our
      happiness, if only he could have been
      present. I am confident that there is not one
      person in this room today who would not
      wish to shake his hand firmly, and wish
      him well.
GROOM: I wish he *were* here. I'd like to shake him
      by the hand for one.
GROOM'S MOTHER:
      So do I.
GROOM'S FATHER:
      Yes.
GROOM'S BROTHER:
      Hear, hear.
STANLEY: Well, ladies and gentlemen, he is here! At
      this moment he is wishing his sister and her
      bridegroom the very best of luck. He hopes
      to be allowed to catch a glimpse of the
      happy couple as we leave—just a glimpse
      from across the street.

133

(STANLEY *sits down. There is a terrible pause.*)
GROOM'S MOTHER:

Mr. Williams, I think you ought to go and fetch him.

(STANLEY'S *eyes swim gratefully at her, then he goes off* R., *coming back almost instantly with* TIM.)

JENNY: Tim!

(*He comes forward hesitantly, shakes hands with* JENNY. *Flash bulbs flash. Cameras click. Everyone rushes forward to greet* TIM. *He takes a glass of champagne, and toasts the happy couple.*)

TIM: To the bride and groom.

(*Confusion. Cameras. Cries of* "Hear, hear", "Well said." "Well done, old man." *Someone starts to sing* "For he's a jolly good fellow". JENNY *hands him a rose.*)

JENNY: You see the colour?

BRIDE'S FATHER:

"Foooor he's a jolly good fellow", etc.

(*She is swept off by her groom and guests, her eyes glancing back at* TIM.)

STANLEY: Turner was warmly, fondly welcomed. He shook hands with his sister, the mother of his babies. He shook hands with the bridegroom. Somebody gave him a glass of champagne and he drank the happy couple's health. The best, the newsiest, the most story-telling picture of the year had been obtained for the paper. It was splashed the following Sunday—the picture of the uninvited guest at the wedding of the girl who narried her brother. And that was that.

134

(The stage is clear by now except for the outline of TURNER'S *house. It is dark.)*
Or that should have been that. That was
nine years ago. And now here I am outside
that little suburban house in Leicester,
waiting for a glimpse of the couple who
have lived there, these past seven years,
never seeing anyone, never even answering
the door, leaving notes for the tradesmen.
I know who the man is; it's Turner all right.
But what about the woman with him,
locked up, day and night? Last week, this
newspaper went to find out. I can now state
quite definitely that the couple living there
in dark seclusion are Timothy Turner and
his sister, Jenny.
(He bawls through the letter box.)
TIM! JENNY! TIM! JENNY! JENNY!
It's only old Stanley. It's your pal, Stanley.
Life hasn't been too good to me either, you
know. Give us a break. Eh, Jenny. Come
on. Be a pal. To old Stan.
(Vexed.)
It's no good hiding, you know. You've got
to come out one day. You've got to come
out one day, and when you do, we'll be
waiting . . . Jenny!
(Slips newspaper through door.)
I put a copy of this issue through the door,
just to show them that the world is still
interested in *them*, and, yes, wants to help.
To Timothy and Jenny I leave this message.
You can't escape the world. Even if you
want to, it won't let you. Come out then,

135

I say. Show yourselves. Be brave. Be
courageous. Fear not. Fear not.
(STANLEY *collapses, drunk and miserable.*
Dead possibly.)

CURTAIN

End of Play